RARE IMAGES OF THE FIRST 100 YEARS

GRAND PRIX!

BY QUENTIN SPURRING

Design by Tom Morgan

DAVID BULL PUBLISHING

Copyright © 2006 by Quentin Spurring and David Bull Publishing. All rights reserved. No part of this book may be used or reproduced in any manner whatsoever without written permission from the Publisher except in the case of brief quotations embodied in critical articles and reviews.

We recognize that some words, model names, and designations mentioned in this book are the property of the trademark holder. We use them only for identification purposes.

Library of Congress Control Number: 2005939004

ISBN: 1 893618 67 6

David Bull Publishing, logo, and colophon are trademarks of David Bull Publishing, Inc.

Book and cover design: Tom Morgan, Blue Design, Portland, Maine

Printed in Hong Kong

10 9 8 7 6 5 4 3 2 1

David Bull Publishing
4250 East Camelback Road
Suite K150
Phoenix, AZ 85018
602-852-9500
602-852-9503 (fax)
www.bullpublishing.com

PAGE 2: A film cameraman takes up an almost suicidal position to capture the start of the 1959 Monaco Grand Prix, showing blind faith in Jack Brabham as he trails pole position winner Stirling Moss in Rob Walker's Cooper and Jean Behra (Ferrari 246) off the line. Coming up behind are Tony Brooks (Ferrari), Joakim Bonnier (BRM P25), Phil Hill (Ferrari), Maurice Trintignant in Rob Walker's second Cooper, and Bruce McLaren in the second works Cooper. Brabham battled with Moss and Behra and, after both had retired, held off a late charge by Brooks.

PAGE 3: Jody Scheckter drives down the hill from the Station Hairpin towards Portier during a dominant performance in the 1979 Monaco Grand Prix. Scheckter put this flat-12 Ferrari 312T4 on the pole and led every one of the 76 laps, finishing under challenge from Clay Regazzoni's Williams FW07, which was less than half a second behind after coming through the field from 16th on the grid.

RIGHT: Monaco race director Charles Faroux liked wearing plus-fours, but the drivers still took him seriously. Here he briefs the cream of 1935 Grand Prix racing (except the Auto Union drivers, who missed this race): left to right, Philippe "Phi-Phi" Etancelin (about to drive a Maserati), Antonio Brivio, Tazio Nuvolari, René Dreyfus (all Alfa Romeos), Giuseppe Farina (Maserati), Rudi Caracciola (Mercedes-Benz), Earl Howe (Bugatti), Luigi Fagioli (Mercedes), Raymond Sommer obscured by Faroux (Alfa Romeo), and Goffredo Zehender (Maserati). A few minutes later, the often truculent Fagioli, in typical pose with hands on hips as he eyes down an unconcerned Nuvolari, set off to become the first man to score a flag-to-flag victory at Monaco.

FOLLOWING PAGE: Scuderia Ferrari Marlboro mechanics swarm all over Michael Schumacher's F2001 in the Sepang pit lane during the second race of 2001. Having achieved and maintained an exceptional standard of mechanical reliability, Ferrari was now also equipping Schumacher with the fastest car in the field. He came through a heavy midrace rain shower to win the Malaysian Grand Prix from teammate Rubens Barrichello, leaving David Coulthard's third-place McLaren Mercedes almost half a minute behind.

CONTENTS

The first recorded use of the French term "Grand Prix" was in 1721 by the Academie des Sciences in Paris for a scientific prize. It was subsequently used for awards in art, literature, music, and many other human endeavors. In 1863, the title "Grand Prix de Paris" was given to a horse race, and the term was used in equestrian and several other sports thereafter. Automobile racing joined them in 1901, when a French national event over a route known as the Circuit du Sud-Ouest was named the Grand Prix de Pau.

The first international motor race to be given the title Grand Prix was run by the Automobile Club de France over two historic days—June 26–27, 1906—on closed public roads to the east of the city of Le Mans. Thirty-two cars were entered by 12 manufacturers. The winner, after almost 770 miles, was a 90hp Renault, capable of over 90mph and raced on the latest Michelin pneumatic tires by a professional Austro-Hungarian driver by the name of Ferenc Szisz.

Gloire de la France
1895–1906

The 1906 Grand Prix de l'Automobile Club de France (ACF) was 12 years in gestation. France had led the way with the newfangled automobiles. The first genuine race, contested by 22 of them, was a town-to-town event in June 1895, taking competitors 750 miles from Paris to Bordeaux and back. Among its sponsors were two wealthy Americans, James Gordon Bennett and William Kissam Vanderbilt, who both later would have central roles in the development of motor racing. It was organized by an ad hoc committee that evolved into the ACF, which would be the most significant race organizer until long after World War I.

This race attracted enormous public attention in France and made a national hero of Emile Levassor, the first man back in Paris. The nation's ingenious new manufacturers lost no time in introducing developments specifically for racing. It was the ACF that established the first controls over the cars competing in its events. The limitation of performance and costs has been the rationale behind the technical regulations that have governed competition cars of all kinds ever since.

The ACF organized many *ville-à-ville* races at the end of the 19th century, usually starting them from Paris, and most were won by either Panhard-Levassor or Mors. In 1898, the ACF responded to requests to offer separate prizes for smaller cars by creating the first racing categories. The front-

---

OPPOSITE: Maurice Farman slows his 40hp Panhard-Levassor as he approaches the Arras town control on the Circuit du Nord, a route over 536 miles from Paris to Arras and back again. All 36 cars in this ACF-organized race in February 1902, including a Mercedes driven by Willie K. Vanderbilt, had to use fuel based on alcohol, production of which was in surplus in France at the time. It was also the first race held to the ACF's 1000kg formula; to comply, Panhard had shed 300kg from the weight of this four-cylinder, 7.4-liter "Heavy Car." Exactly a year before, Farman had won the eight-car Grand Prix de Pau in southwest France.

running "Heavy Cars" were defined by the club's Commission Sportive as weighing more than 400kg, and awards were also offered for vehicles weighing between 200 and 400kg, between 100 and 200kg, and less than 100kg. No engine restrictions were applied. The first purpose-built racing cars complied with these regulations in the ACF's Paris–Amsterdam–Paris race. The categories were modified in 1901, when the Heavy Cars were given a minimum dry weight of 650kg.

Crowds and dust were always problems in these *ville-á-ville* events and, when a small boy was killed near Reims while watching the 1901 Paris-Berlin, the French government immediately banned the races. However the ACF reached an accommodation with the authorities by offering to experiment with fuel made from alcohol for a race in 1902 between Paris and Arras. A maximum weight of 1000kg was added to the regulations for this event and, as a crowd control measure, it was neutralized by means of time controls as the cars passed through towns. The race passed without major incident. This cleared the way for the ACF to stage a bigger event 4 months later between Paris and Vienna, in which there was a separate class for alcohol-fueled cars.

The ACF went on to use this 1000kg formula for all its races through 1906. The maximum weight limit was a compromise between two factions of the publicity-hungry participating manufacturers. Some had wanted to race with the relatively small engines that were then in production, but others resisted any upper limit, believing that racing should be all about power. The ACF's intention was to encourage all the designers to develop smaller engines to save weight.

Over the first few years of motor sport, the outputs of the race-winning engines increased dramatically, from less than 5hp in 1895 to 85hp in 1903. Speeds rose from 20mph to 80mph. The epic town-to-town races came to an abrupt end when the ACF's Paris-Madrid event that May, which had more than 270 entries and was witnessed by an estimated two million people, was halted at Bordeaux after at least eight fatalities, including that of Marcel Renault in a car of his own make. Up to that point, the 70hp Mors of race leader Fernand Gabriel had averaged 40mph on the dusty, unpaved roads.

All the major European governments immediately banned racing on public highways. However, two initiatives had already laid the foundations for the first Grand Prix and all motor racing ever since.

Late in 1899, James Gordon Bennett, the proprietor of the *New York Herald* and the Paris-based newspaper that would become the *International Herald Tribune,* had offered a magnificent silver trophy. His Coupe Internationale was to be awarded annually to three-car national teams contesting a single race, and each winning nation was to host the event the following year. The Coupe took 3 years to establish itself, during which only the French industry took it seriously. In 1903, however, it was staged as a stand-alone race on a closed course only 5 weeks after the horrors of the Paris-Madrid. It abruptly caught the imagination of the media and the public, and the result boosted sales of Daimler's race-winning Mercedes brand.

The commercial impact of the Mercedes victory created a specific problem for the ACF, which hitherto had selected its three-car team. As the cradle of motoring, France had many more manufacturers than any other

ABOVE: Only the national motoring associations of Britain and France entered teams for the 1902 Gordon Bennett Cup, so it was run in conjunction with the ACF's Paris-Vienna race, which had 137 starters. Here Britain's Selwyn Edge (in the car) and his cousin and riding mechanic, Cecil Edge (standing to Selwyn's left), prepare for the early morning start at Champigny. Their new "armored wood" Napier chassis, weighing 67kg less than the 1000kg maximum, was powered by a four-cylinder, 6.4-liter engine producing 45bhp. The six Coupe competitors were classified when they reached their allocated race distance at Innsbruck, where the Napier was the last one standing.

OPPOSITE: Napier's 1902 victory obliged Britain, where road racing was prohibited, to stage the 1903 Coupe Internationale. It was held over a figure-eight circuit of closed public roads near Ballyshannon in Ireland: 3 laps of a 40-mile loop and 4 laps of a 52-mile loop, with a common home straight. Three-car teams were entered by America, Britain, France, and Germany, each presenting its cars in a national color (respectively green, blue, white, and red). The crowd is watching one of three 9.2-liter, four-cylinder Mercedes 60 touring cars, hastily pressed into service after a fire had destroyed Daimler's new 90hp racing cars. Camille Jenatzy's victory had an immediate impact on Mercedes sales.

ABOVE: Seven nations participated in the 1904 Coupe Internationale over 4 laps of a 79-mile circuit near Bad Homburg, in the Taunus Mountains of Germany, where France regained the trophy. Léon Théry's Richard-Brasier, its four-cylinder, 9.8-liter engine developing 96bhp at 1300rpm, is pictured at the start. Nicknamed "The Chronometer" for his consistency, or more popularly "Mort Aux Vaches" after he killed a cow during the 1903 Circuit des Ardennes, Théry won a famous duel with "Red Devil" Camille Jenatzy's Mercedes 90. Théry and Brasier won the Coupe again when it was run for the last time near Clermont-Ferrand in 1905, with FIAT's Felice Nazzaro and Alessandro Cagno second and third.

nation, so the selection had always been controversial. Ultimately it was the dissatisfaction of the ambitious but unrepresented French companies that led the ACF to replace the Coupe with the first Grand Prix.

In July 1902, the first closed circuit was established in Belgium not only as a crowd control measure, but also as a means of resolving timekeeping problems associated with neutralizing the *ville-à-ville* races when the route included towns. The Circuit des Ardennes used closed public roads over an 85.34km (53-mile) route based on the town of Bastogne. The inaugural, 6-lap race received 75 entries and pointed the way forward.

In June 1904, 13 national clubs—those in America, Austria, Belgium, Britain, Denmark, France, Germany, Holland, Italy, Portugal, Russia, Spain, and Switzerland—got together to found the first international body. They named it the Association Internationale des Automobile Clubs Reconnus (AIACR) and adopted the ACF's 1000kg formula, which had already been used by other race organizers. But the ACF's efforts to lobby its fellow AIACR members for a change in the Coupe sporting regulations were in vain.

In October of that year, businessman and philanthropist Willie K. Vanderbilt established another major event for the 1000kg racing cars in America. All manufacturers were welcome to compete for the inaugural Vanderbilt Cup on Long Island, New York, and this served to increase the pressure from the French industry. The race was won by a Panhard-Levassor driven by expatriate American George Heath. It was one of three shipped across the Atlantic to challenge American works teams from Packard, Pope, and Royal. Also from France, Clément-Bayard sent out one car, while De Dietrich and Renault were represented by U.S.-owned cars, as were FIAT and Mercedes.

The pressure told on the ACF. The organization announced that, in addition to the 1905 Coupe, it would organize an entirely new race in which France would be permitted to enter 18 cars, Britain and Germany 6 each, and all other nations 3. And it put up a "grand prix" for this event of FF 100,000—equivalent to about EUR €335,000 (US$260,000) today. It was a substantially bigger incentive than the Coupe Internationale.

The other AIACR member clubs were not impressed. After a stormy meeting in Berlin, the ACF reluctantly canceled the 1905 Grand Prix but asserted that, whatever the outcome of the Coupe, it would not host, organize, or support that event in 1906. Instead, it prepared for its new Grand Prix. Like the Vanderbilt Cup, this was declared open to teams of up to three cars from any manufacturer, with no national prize.

ABOVE: Clifford Earp halts his 90hp Napier, streamlined for racing with a wraparound tubular radiator, at a town control during the last Gordon Bennett race. At least one Napier contested every Coupe Internationale from 1901 on and, after Earp had won an elimination race on the Isle of Man, this six-cylinder, 15-liter L48 was in the 1905 Great Britain and Ireland team with two Wolseleys. The 100mph Napier's two-speed gearbox turned out to be a severe handicap on the mountainous Circuit d'Auvergne, an 85-mile course laid out by Michelin near its factory at Clermont-Ferrand. However, the team survived intact, with Charles Rolls eighth, Earp ninth, and Cecil Bianchi eleventh of the 12 finishers.

CHAPTER 1
The Titans
1906–1914

The entry for the first Grand Prix in June 1906 justified the ACF's assessment of the importance of the French automobile industry and its decision to abandon the Gordon Bennett Cup. The event included seven three-car French teams, from Brasier, Darracq, Hotchkiss, Lorraine-Dietrich, Panhard-Levassor, and Renault, which won with Ferenc Szisz. These 21 cars were backed up by singleton entries from Gobron-Brillié and Grégoire. No British cars were entered, Germany offered only one three-car team (Mercedes), and Italy two (Itala and FIAT, which finished second with Felice Nazzaro).

That October, 250,000 Americans watched the top European factories and drivers dominate the Vanderbilt Cup on Long Island. Louis Wagner (Darracq) won from Vincenzo Lancia (FIAT), Arthur Duray (Lorraine-Dietrich), Albert Clément (Clément-Bayard), Camille Jenatzy (Mercedes), Nazzaro (FIAT), and Alessandro Cagno (Itala). It was the last international race held to the AIACR-sanctioned 1000kg formula.

The 5-year-old regulations were dropped because some of the manufacturers had built their chassis even lighter to fit them with even heavier, even bigger, and even less efficient engines. Their designers, interested only in brute horsepower, had simply ignored "the spirit of the regulations." Only one car (the 7.4-liter Grégoire) had used an engine smaller than 12 liters in the Grand Prix, for which Panhard had produced a new four-cylinder of more than 18 liters.

OPPOSITE: Ferenc Szisz joined Renault in 1900 and was soon appointed to lead its testing department. In 1902, he became Louis Renault's riding mechanic in town-to-town events. Renault withdrew from racing after Marcel Renault's death in the 1903 Paris-Madrid but returned in 1905, when Szisz was one of its drivers. He failed to qualify in the French elimination trial for the Coupe Internationale, and he was placed fifth when the Vanderbilt Cup in New York was stopped due to a crowd invasion. His 1906 victory made "Feri" a big star in France and he finished second a year later in Dieppe. In 1908 he was running third in the Grand Prix when halted by a tire failure, and second in the American Grand Prize at Savannah when stopped by a collapsed wheel bearing. Renault then pulled out of racing, and he left the company. Szisz was injured while competing for Alda in the Grand Prix in 1914, when he scored his last victory at Anjou, driving a Lorraine-Dietrich with an arm in plaster. Having taken French nationality, he was an army volunteer in World War I, worked for the Breugeot aircraft factory until his retirement, and died in France in 1944, at age 71. His grave is still tended by Renault and the ACF.

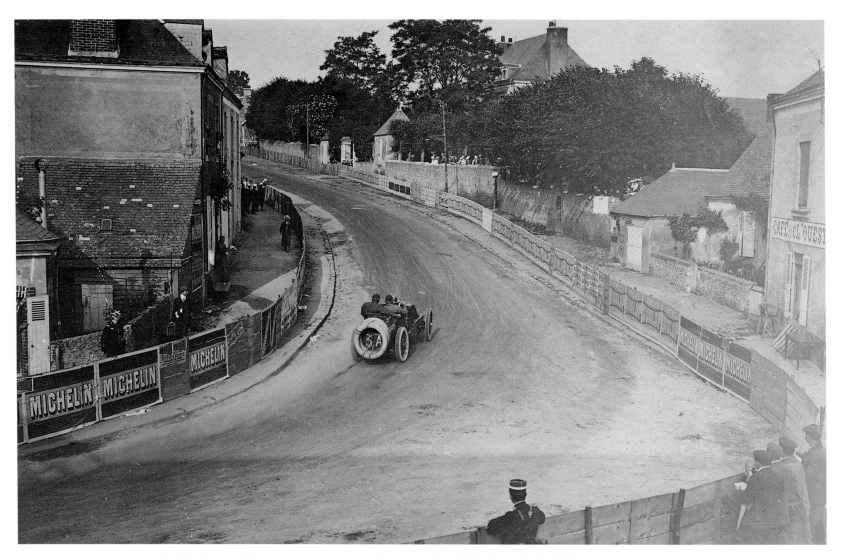

Pending international agreement on a replacement Grand Prix formula, the ACF ran its 1907 event near Dieppe to fuel consumption rules, which were enforced by sealing the fuel tanks. The Vanderbilt Cup was not held in 1907 after inadequate spectator control on the Long Island circuit had finally had fatal consequences the year before.

A fortnight after Nazzaro and Fiat (which dropped the capitals from its name that year) had defeated Szisz and Renault in the 1907 Grand Prix, the AIACR was convened in Ostend, Belgium, to establish a new international formula. It followed a lead set in Germany for the new Kaiserpreis by combining a minimum weight with engine restrictions, although it fell short of limiting displacement. This Ostend Formula placed restrictions on bore diameters. Challenged to derive the maximum power from a given piston area, the engineers had to look beyond volume, and saw rpm. They began to accelerate crankshaft speeds from as slow as 800rpm to well over 2000rpm. Top speeds crept past 100mph.

The 1908 Grand Prix at Dieppe produced a 1-2-3 for German manufacturers, with a 12.8-liter Mercedes, driven by Christian Lautenschlager, leading Benz drivers Victor Héméry and René Hanriot.

Under pressure from its own entrants, the American Automobile Association (AAA) did not adopt the new AIACR formula, implementing a 1200kg maximum weight regulation for the 1908 Vanderbilt Cup. This was an

ABOVE: Steam and smoke from the four-cylinder, 14.4-liter Mercedes 120 accompany Camille Jenatzy, Daimler's 1903 Gordon Bennett winner, to the start of the 1906 Grand Prix. Five years before, Mercedes had introduced innovations including the steel chassis, the honeycomb radiator, and mechanically operated inlet valves, but it was no longer a front-runner. In the race, Jenatzy's eyes were damaged by swirls of road dust and he was placed 16th at the end of the first day. The rules allowed a change of driver, and the car was taken over by Alexander Burton, who was soon hit in the eye by a stone thrown up by another car. He managed to finish 10th.

OPPOSITE: Ferenc Szisz swings his 13-liter Renault AK through the village of Connerré during his winning drive in the first Grand Prix de l'ACF, staged to the east of Le Mans over 2 days in June 1906. Six laps were completed each day of a 64.1-mile course, for a total of more than 769 miles, and the cars were locked up overnight in a floodlit *parc fermé*. The Renaults, FIATs, and Clément-Bayards were built light enough to fit Michelin's new detachable wheel/tire assemblies, each of which weighed 9kg, and remain under the 1000kg weight limit. This allowed these manufacturers to gain substantial time during pit stops. Renault used the Michelin *jantes amovibles* at the front only, but Szisz's pacy and consistent driving took him into the lead on the third lap from Vincenzo Lancia's 130bhp FIAT. His car's mechanical reliability kept him there for the duration, through 19 changes of rim. After Lancia was delayed, FIAT's baton was taken up by Felice Nazzaro, who narrowly beat Albert Clément into third place—both men had chosen not to use Michelin's new equipment.

opportunity for the Automobile Club of America, the AIACR-recognized body, which planned an alternative event for the European teams. The inaugural American Grand Prize at Savannah in 1908 was contested by Clément-Bayard, Benz, Fiat (which won with Wagner), Itala, Lorraine-Dietrich, and Renault, and four American companies, Acme, Buick, Chadwick (the firm that raced the first supercharged racing engine), and National.

Five weeks before this race, the AIACR had again convened in Ostend to agree on a Grand Prix formula for 1909. The delegates voted to reduce the maximum weight to 900kg and the bore diameters by 17%. This formula was never used; the European manufacturers now regarded racing costs as prohibitive. At the 1908 Paris Show, 17 signed a bond to abstain, led by the French companies that had been humiliated in Dieppe by their German rivals. The ACF announced that its 1909 Grand Prix would be staged under the new AIACR regulations near Anjou—but added a stipulation that the event would be canceled if fewer than 40 entries were received. At the December 31, 1908, closing date, there were 9.

The ACA did not stage its American Grand Prize in 1909, either, and the AAA implemented a 600cid maximum engine swept volume for its Vanderbilt Cup. This brought it into line with the rules used for the races that would evolve into the AAA National Championship, devised primarily for American production engines (which would endure until 1955). The decision effectively removed the United States from international collaboration in motor racing until after World War I.

LEFT: Arthur Duray's 18.1-liter Lorraine-Dietrich passes the main grandstands on a straight near Montfort after stopping at its "depot" (pit) during the 1906 Grand Prix. Duray was never a contender, finishing a distant eighth. Six weeks later, however, he won the next 1000kg race with this 130hp car on the Circuit des Ardennes in Belgium, and he was third in the Vanderbilt Cup on Long Island, New York, that closed the formula. Duray and Lorraine-Dietrich also won a last vestige of *ville-à-ville* racing when a race was run from Moscow to St. Petersburg in 1907. He then led the Grand Prix at Dieppe until a gearbox failure intervened.

The ACF was unable to revive its race in either 1910 or 1911. However the Automobile Club de l'Ouest, which had run the 1906 race at Le Mans for the ACF, gained the support of its national body in 1911 to hold a race it called the Grand Prix de France. It was contested by a variety of cars including former Grand Prix racers, and cynics called it the "Grand Prix des Vieux Tacots" (Grand Prix of Old Crocks). But the success of this race, won by Héméry's Fiat, prompted the ACF to try again in 1912.

Cautious lest it receive another small entry, the ACF drew up simple regulations stipulating only a maximum vehicle width, with which all the numerous voiturettes complied. These popular 800kg cars, racing under formulas first devised by *L'Auto* magazine in 1906, were now powered by 3000cc engines. No fewer than 34 were raced against 13 Grand Prix cars, and the event, in Dieppe again, was won by Georges Boillot's groundbreaking, twin-camshaft Peugeot, designed by former Hispano-Suiza engineer Ernest Henry.

For the 1913 Grand Prix at Amiens, the ACF created another "fuel formula," more demanding than the 1907 requirement, and combined it with weight definitions. Peugeot was on a high, Jules Goux having humbled Mercedes, Mercer, Stutz, and Sunbeam in the third Indianapolis 500 6 weeks before. The team suffered a dreadful blow when its chief engineer and third driver, Paul Zuccarelli, who had come with Henry from Hispano-Suiza, was one of two fatalities during practice. But it secured a 1-2 with Boillot and Goux, ahead of Delage's voiturettes.

The ACF involved the manufacturers and other organizers in determining a 4.5-liter formula for 1914, and the response was extremely positive: 37 entries from 13 factory teams. The Royal Automobile Club de Belgique, the Automobilclub von Deutschland and the Automobile Club d'Italia announced that they would use this new formula to stage their own Grands Prix, and the Italian race was scheduled for September.

The 1914 race in Lyons included new, purpose-built racing cars from Peugeot and Mercedes. The Peugeots were hampered by tire problems, and Mercedes achieved a 1-2-3. Silence greeted the German cars as they crossed the line. Only 17 days earlier, the heir to the Austrian throne, Archduke Franz Ferdinand, had been assassinated in Sarajevo (in an Austro-Daimler reputedly chauffeured by works Mercedes racing driver Otto Merz). Within 3 weeks, Germany and France would be at war.

GRAND PRIX REGULATIONS

1906 *ACF Grand Prix formula. Engines: free. Dry weight: 650kg (1432lb) minimum, 1000kg (2204lb) maximum, without lubricants, fuel, water, fenders, tools, spare wheels and other parts, upholstery, and lamps. Allowance of 7kg (15lb) for cars with magneto ignitions.* **1907** *ACF Grand Prix formula. Engines: free. Weight: free. Minimum fuel consumption: 30 liters/100km (9.4mpg).* **1908** *AIACR Grand Prix formula. Engine cylinder bore diameter maximums: 310mm for single-cylinder engines, 219mm for two-cylinder, 179mm for three-cylinder, 155mm for four-cylinder, 127mm for six-cylinder, 110mm for eight-cylinder. Minimum dry weight: 1100kg (2425lb), including lubricants.* **1912** *ACF Grand Prix formula. Engines: free. Weight: free. Maximum vehicle width: 1750mm.* **1913** *ACF Grand Prix formula. Engines: free. Dry weight: 800kg (1763lb) minimum, 1100kg (2425lb) maximum. Minimum fuel consumption: 30 liters/100km (14.12mpg). Streamlined tails banned.* **1914** *ACF Grand Prix formula. Engine piston displacement: 4500cc maximum. Dry weight: 800kg (1763lb) minimum, 1100kg (2425lb) maximum.*

ABOVE: This four-cylinder, 12.9-liter, 100bhp Clément-Bayard, driven by "De la Touloubre" (real name Gentil), was out of the 1906 Grand Prix with a broken gearbox after only 3 laps, but the team's lead entry, driven by 21-year-old Albert Clément, completed the race and finished third. The son of Adolphe Clément, the firm's founder, Albert was its top driver but was killed during an unofficial practice run for the 1907 Grand Prix on the Circuit de la Seine Inférieure near Dieppe. These French cars were built under license in Britain under the Talbot brand name starting in 1903. After World War I, the marque effectively became part of the Sunbeam-Talbot-Darracq combine.

ABOVE: Second with Felice Nazzaro in the 1905 Coupe Internationale and the 1906 Grand Prix, Fiat built three different engines in 1907 to comply with the regulations for the Targa Florio in Sicily, the Kaiserpreis in Germany, and the Grand Prix in France. Nazzaro, Fiat's ace driver, achieved an astonishing clean sweep by winning all three. This is the "fuel formula" Grand Prix car, powered by a 15.3-liter, four-cylinder engine developing 130bhp at 1600rpm. Benefiting from the gearbox failure that halted Arthur Duray's Lorraine-Dietrich 2 laps from the end, Nazzaro won from Ferenc Szisz's 12.8-liter Renault—the defending champion misjudged his consumption and had fuel to spare at the finish.

ABOVE LEFT: Peugeot entered a team of three trail-blazing new cars for the 1912 Grand Prix, held over 2 days on a 47.8-mile course to the northeast of Dieppe that included a purpose-built stadium area on the city outskirts. Peugeot had become dominant in voiturette racing, and the new L76 established a very high new standard. Powered by a 7.6-liter, four-cylinder engine with two overhead camshafts and 16 valves producing 120bhp at 2200rpm, the 1400kg Peugeot had quick-change wheel rims and was refueled from a hose under pressure, whereas its opposition all used churns. Only George Boillot's L76 finished, but it was leading by 13 minutes.

ABOVE RIGHT: The main opposition to Peugeot's innovative new cars at Dieppe in 1912 came from Fiat with three of its S74 racing cars, powered by 14.1-liter, four-cylinder SOHC engines. David Bruce-Brown, Fiat's 1911 American Grand Prize winner with an S74, was in the lead at the end of the first day but was then stopped by a split fuel line; he repaired it but was disqualified after borrowing fuel to get back to the pits. Fellow American Ralph DePalma (pictured) was also disqualified for receiving outside assistance, and Louis Wagner's S74 was a distant second. DePalma went on to win the Vanderbilt Cup at the end of the season with a Mercedes.

OPPOSITE: The 1906 Grand Prix winner, Ferenc Szisz, prepares to take the start of the 1914 race at Lyons at the wheel of an Alda, built for the 4.5-liter formula by a company founded by former driver Fernand Charron. The winner of the first Coupe Internationale in 1900 had invited the readers of *L'Auto* magazine to name the car, and the acronym he had chosen stood for "Ah, La Délicieuse Automobile!" In the race, Szisz's arm was broken in the pits by the white car at right, an Opel en route to 10th place driven by Carl Jörns. Only 18 days later, Szisz won a race at Anjou with a Lorraine-Dietrich.

OPPOSITE: Georges Boillot, Peugeot's Grand Prix winner in 1912 and 1913, undertakes a pit stop during the 1914 race on the Lyons-Givors circuit, which was watched by 300,000 people. Three of these EX5 racing cars were opposed by five Mercedes, all purpose-built for the 4.5-liter formula. The Peugeot had an innovative four-wheel braking system and a four-cylinder DOHC engine that matched the output of the Mercedes 18/100. Boillot was confident of his hat trick, but the best drive of his career ended in a tearful failure. It was his last race. As a wartime fighter ace, he was fatally engaged by five Fokker pilots in a dogfight over Verdun in 1916.

ABOVE: Christian Lautenschlager heads for his second Grand Prix victory, in 1914 at Lyons with riding mechanic Hans Sieger. Their new, coil-sprung Mercedes 18/100 had an SOHC engine developing 110bhp at 3200rpm—double the crankshaft speed of any previous Daimler engine. Max Sailer's sister car shot into the lead soon after the staggered start with Georges Boillot's Peugeot EX5 in hot pursuit. Sailer's engine broke a conrod on the 6th of the 20 laps, but Boillot could not resist Lautenschlager's pass 2 laps out from the finish. The Peugeot's engine broke a valve on the last 23-mile lap, and Louis Wagner and Otto Salzer made it a 1-2-3 for Mercedes.

2

CHAPTER 2

The Roaring Twenties
1921–1927

World War I devastated the European automobile industry, and the first major postwar race was in the United States. The Indianapolis 500 had been held in 1915 and 1916 (shortened to 300 miles), and had been won respectively by a Mercedes and a Peugeot built for the 1914 Grand Prix. The 1919 event, subtitled "Victory Sweepstakes," was significant for the debut of straight-eight DOHC racing engines designed in France by Ernest Henry for Ballot and by Harry Miller in America for Duesenberg. The inspiration for both was a wartime aero V16, designed by Ettore Bugatti and manufactured by Duesenberg for America's war effort.

France lifted a postwar ban on racing in August 1920, when the Coupe des Voiturettes was run at Le Mans, and in 1921 the ACF implemented a new, voiturette-based, 3-liter Grand Prix formula that had already been anticipated at Indianapolis. Ballot and Duesenberg downsized their straight-eights and competed both in America and in the first postwar Grand Prix at Le Mans.

In 1922, the AIACR formed a subcommittee to govern motor racing. The first members of its Commission Sportive Internationale (CSI) were delegates from Austria, Belgium, Britain, France, Italy, and the United States, and their first act was to implement a 2-liter Grand Prix formula. Six manufacturers built cars in 1922, and four more in 1923, when the AIACR held its first International Calendar Congress in Paris and announced the first Manufacturers championship for 1925. Riding mechanics were eliminated for safety reasons in the final year of the 2-liter formula, and Grand Prix racing began to take a form that we can recognize today. Certainly the thinking of the CSI that year is familiar: the new supercharging technology boosted power outputs to 200bhp and top speeds to 140mph, so a 500cc reduction was adopted for 1926–27.

OPPOSITE: Two of the A22 racing cars built by French manufacturer Rolland-Pilain are presented for inspection in the Strasbourg scrutineering enclosure before being driven by Albert Guyot (foreground) and Louis Wagner in the 1922 Grand Prix de l'ACF. Both these 2-liter straight-eight cars were parked after only 2 laps on race day, smitten by engine failures, but the company was more competitive in 1923. Emile Pilain deployed a hydraulic braking system under Duesenberg license, and Guyot led Gaston Delalande in a 1-2 against weak opposition in the very wet San Sebastian Grand Prix in Spain. On this relatively high note, Rolland-Pilain quit top-level racing.

France lost its monopoly on the term "Grand Prix" when the inaugural Italian Grand Prix was run in 1921 on a road course at Montichiari, near Brescia, before the purpose-built Autodromo Nazionale at Monza was opened in 1922. Spain added two new races in 1923, on a road circuit at Lasarte, San Sebastian, and a concrete speedway at Sitges, near Barcelona. Spa-Francorchamps hosted the first Belgian Grand Prix in 1925, and Brooklands (built back in 1907) was the scene of Britain's first Grand Prix, in 1926. The Montlhéry speedway near Paris was completed in 1924, and the Nürburgring road circuit in 1927.

Few manufacturers that had contested the 1914 Grand Prix survived the war. One that did was Peugeot, one of whose prewar 4.9-liter Grand Prix racers again won the Indy 500 in 1919. Peugeot attempted a comeback there in 1920 with a team of advanced new cars, but their 3-liter, four-cylinder, 20-valve engines all broke. Peugeot withdrew—and stayed away for the next 74 years.

Comebacks by Mercedes and Benz were also brief. German manufacturers (and drivers) were initially banned from racing by the European nations that had prevailed in the war. America was more forgiving. Mercedes returned in 1922 at Indianapolis, racing four-cylinder Targa Florio cars equipped with superchargers. It then contested the 1924 Italian Grand Prix with its blown, 32-valve, straight-eight M218 engine, putting 170bhp at 7000rpm through a chassis designed by freelance engineer Ferdinand Porsche. Four of these 130mph cars were entered, but Count Louis Zborowski was killed midway through the race, and the others were withdrawn. Thereafter the M218 was only raced in Germany.

In the meantime, two entries from Benz were accepted by the Monza organizers for their 1923 Grand Prix, and the first mid-engined, inboard-braked racing cars caused a sensation. One of these innovative straight-six cars finished fourth. Germany was not readmitted to the AIACR until 1925, the year before Daimler merged with Benz, and the Mercedes M218 won Formule Libre races on the AVUS (the inaugural German Grand Prix) with Rudi Caracciola and at Solitude with Otto Merz. The mid-engine concept was not adopted by the expanded company.

Of the other prewar participants, Fiat, Clément-Talbot, Darracq, Sunbeam, and Delage all raced again in the 1920s, and all had success in turn. With a straight-eight equipped with two Roots-type superchargers, the 135mph Fiat 805 was the first car to win a Grand Prix with a forced induction engine, in a 1-2 at Monza in

ABOVE: "It's a Duesey!" French officials look on in huddled dismay as riding mechanic Ernie Olsen raises an arm in triumph and Jimmy Murphy drives for the line in the first postwar Grand Prix, at Le Mans in 1921. The 3-liter, straight-eight, 115bhp Duesenberg 183 was the first racing car equipped with hydraulic brakes. The system, pressurized by a mixture of glycerine and water, had been devised after a defeat by a four-wheel-braked Ballot in a race at Elgin, Chicago, the previous year. Ballot's unexpected defeat on its home turf was shamefully greeted with boos from the crowd and no national anthem was played.

1923. Three of the other companies were reborn after the war as elements of a new conglomerate, Sunbeam-Talbot-Darracq, and returned to competition in 1921 with an unsuccessful 3-liter straight-eight. This was replaced by an underpowered four-cylinder in 1922 before a six-cylinder Fiat 805 copy delivered success for STD in 1923.

However the decade most notably marked the arrival of two powerful new racing marques: first Bugatti, which had raced voiturettes before the war, and then Alfa Romeo, the ambitious new company created by Nicola Romeo out of ALFA, which had not had time to complete a 4.5-liter Grand Prix project initiated in 1914. Alfa Romeo intended to enter Grand Prix racing in 1923 with its blown straight-six "P1" designed by former Fiat engineer Luigi Bazzi, but it was never raced after a practice accident at Monza killed Ugo Sivocci. Over the next winter, Enzo Ferrari of Alfa Corse also prized Vittorio Jano away from Fiat, and his "P2" set the standard in 1924–25.

Across the Atlantic, the AAA complied as closely as practicable with the AIACR regulations, but European participations at Indianapolis in 1921 (by Ballot and Sunbeam), 1923 (Bugatti and Mercedes), and 1925 (Fiat) all failed, and neither Duesenberg nor Miller was able to repeat the shock 1921 result at Le Mans. Miller contested two Grands Prix on European speedways in 1923. Duesenberg was a contender for the 1925 AIACR Manufacturers title, and both companies staged another European foray to Monza in 1927. But the two continents were steadily moving apart in their approaches to motor racing.

Through 1925, technical innovation induced by war found its expression in Grand Prix racing, as commercial optimism induced by peace created new enterprises eager to prove themselves on the racetrack. The United States apart, Grand Prix racing became genuinely international, going from zero to a new zenith, with the straight-eight engine at its core. But the 1926–27 formula was much less successful, coinciding with a dreadful world financial recession. Race promoters adopted the free Formule Libre format to attract enough cars, and the AIACR's attempts to impose new regulations were largely ignored.

GRAND PRIX REGULATIONS

1921 *ACF Grand Prix formula. Engine piston displacement: 3000cc maximum. Dry weight: 800kg (1763lb) minimum.*
1922–25 *AIACR Grand Prix formula. Engine piston displacement: 2000cc maximum. Dry weight: 650kg (1433lb) minimum. Combined weight of driver/riding mechanic: 120kg (264lb) minimum. Body width: 800mm minimum. Rear overhang (behind rear axle centerline): 1500mm maximum. Rearview mirror mandatory.* **1924** *Fuel: increased alcohol content.* **1925** *Riding mechanics banned. Midrace repairs/replenishments to be carried out only by driver and one mechanic.* **1926–27** *AIACR Grand Prix formula. Engine piston displacement: 1500cc maximum. Dry weight: 600kg (1323lb) minimum.* **1927** *Dry weight: 650kg (1433lb) minimum.*

AIACR WORLD CHAMPIONSHIP OF MANUFACTURERS

1925	Alfa Romeo
1926	Bugatti
1927	Delage

OPPOSITE: Henry Segrave and his riding mechanic both remonstrate with Jimmy Murphy for partially blocking their exit from the Talbot pit during the 1921 Grand Prix, which was run on the original version of the circuit that became the venue for the Le Mans 24 Hours. Murphy had a massive accident on the Circuit de la Sarthe during practice a week before this race, sustaining internal injuries, but he discharged himself from the hospital 2 hours before the start, bandaged from waist to shoulders, and secured a heroic, 78mph victory despite two punctures and a holed radiator. The other Duesenberg is André Dubonnet's, which went on to finish fourth.

ABOVE: Fiat managing director Guido Fornaca assembled an outstanding engineering team for its return in 1921, with a 3-liter, short-stroke straight-eight that revved to 4250rpm and has been described as the first high-speed racing engine. It was replaced in 1922 by a 2-liter straight-six with hemispherical-topped cylinders, delivering 100bhp at 4500rpm to the Fiat 804. Here is the team prior to the 1922 Grand Prix at Strasbourg (left to right): debutant Biagio Nazzaro, his accomplished uncle Felice Nazzaro, and Pietro Bordino, who won on Italy's brand-new Autodromo Nazionale at Monza later that season. This extremely effective car was copied by every European racing car manufacturer for years to come.

ABOVE LEFT: The 500-mile 1922 Grand Prix de l'ACF was the first race with a massed start. Biagio Nazzaro (nearest camera) set off toward the back of the 18-car field but, after 15 laps of the 8.3-mile Strasbourg circuit, he was at the back of a Fiat 1-2-3 as the 804 dominated the latest cars from Aston Martin, Ballot, Bugatti, Rolland-Pilain, and Sunbeam. Felice Nazzaro repeated his 1907 victory in the ACF's event, but it was joyless. Nine laps from the finish, a rear axle casting failed on his nephew's car and sent it into a fatal crash. A similar structural failure 7 laps later caused Pietro Bordino also to crash, without injury.

ABOVE RIGHT: Giulio Foresti's Ballot 2LS is refueled during the company's final Grand Prix at Strasbourg in 1922, which none of its three cars finished. Ballot's racing ambitions were thwarted by bad luck and never fulfilled. The manufacturer never won at Indy, and a 1-2 by Jules Goux and Jean Chassagne in the first Italian Grand Prix, after tire problems had hampered the faster Fiats, was its only success in Europe. Ballot equipped its Grand Prix car with streamlined bodywork for this race, housing a spare wheel in its bulbous nose. Otherwise, the 2LS was similar mechanically to the four-cylinder car that had finished third at Le Mans in 1921.

ABOVE: The great Felice Nazzaro endures the rain in the cockpit of his Fiat 804 before his tragic victory in the 1922 Grand Prix. The axle case on his winning car was also found to be cracked when inspected after the finish. As a young FIAT apprentice, Nazzaro was sent to Sicily to prepare racing cars for Vincenzo Florio (the founder of the Targa Florio), and he took up driving, winning consistently for FIAT between 1900 and 1908. He became a constructor, winning both the Targa Florio and Coppa Florio in 1913 with his own Nazzaro cars. He returned to Fiat after the war and won at Strasbourg at the age of 42.

ABOVE: STD's French racing boss, Louis Coatalen, headhunted Fiat engineer Vincenzo Bertarione to design a 2-liter straight-six racer for 1923. Unashamedly based on the cars that had set the pace in 1922, these naturally aspirated, 100bhp Sunbeams were disparagingly nicknamed "the green Fiats." Here are Henry Segrave (at left) and Albert Divo before their 1-2 in the 1923 Grand Prix de l'ACF at Tours, secured after the Fiats' vane-type superchargers had been damaged by dust ingested from the road surface. To complete STD's day, Kenelm Lee Guinness also finished in the team's other car, although hampered by a slipping clutch that put it behind Ernest Friedrich's third-place Bugatti 32.

OPPOSITE: Bugatti came with aerodynamic experimentation when it entered Grand Prix racing in 1922 with its barrel-bodied, straight-eight type 30 finishing 2-3 at Strasbourg. The Bugatti 32 had "tank" bodywork enclosing its wheels when it finished third at Tours in 1923. After producing two of the ugliest racing cars ever seen, Ettore Bugatti then transformed the aesthetics of Grand Prix racing in 1924 when he revealed the handsome, straight-eight Bugatti 35. Five of the brand-new cars made their debut in the 1924 race at Lyons and attracted huge interest. Here Pierre de Vizcaya emerges from the throng around the team to present his 35 to the scrutineers.

OPPOSITE: Ernest Friedrich (right) and Leonico Garnier make pit stops during the 1924 Grand Prix de l'ACF, headed for 8th and 11th places respectively on the debut of the Bugatti 35. Three of the new cars finished the race, but the naturally aspirated, 90bhp 35 was not competitive with the supercharged Alfa Romeos, Delages, and Fiats. Shortly afterward, however, Bugatti offered Grand Prix cars for sale to privateers. Technically, the first "customer" race car was that year's Miller 122, of which 15 were built, but the total production run of the Bugatti 35 series eventually ran to almost 350. These cars won more than 1500 events between 1924 and 1927.

ABOVE: Dario Resta prepares for the 1924 Grand Prix de l'ACF in STD's latest Sunbeam, its straight-six now supercharged and producing 140bhp. Italian-born, English-raised Resta had finished fifth, sixth, and fifth again for Sunbeam in the 1912, 1913, and 1914 Grands Prix. He had then made his name in America with Peugeots, winning 10 races including the American Grand Prize in 1915 and the Indy 300 in 1916, and the Vanderbilt Cup in both years. His career had been destroyed by war, and his comeback here produced 10th place. A month after this photograph was taken, he was killed when a tire blew during a record attempt at Brooklands.

ABOVE LEFT: Delage returned in 1923 with a superb 60deg V12, and recruited Albert Divo from STD to lead its team in 1924. Divo is pictured racing his Delage 2LCV toward a strong second position behind Giuseppe Campari's Alfa Romeo P2 in the 500-mile Grand Prix de l'ACF at Lyons, which used part of the scenic circuit on which the famous 1914 race had been held. The following season, a third, twin-supercharged iteration of the Delage V12, designed by Albert Lory, delivered almost 200bhp at 6500rpm—the best power output achieved under the 2-liter formula—and Divo won the Grands Prix at Montlhéry, France, and Lasarte, Spain.

ABOVE RIGHT: Pietro Bordino leads at Lyons in 1924 with the Fiat 805, designed by Vittorio Jano around a blown straight-eight developing 130bhp at 5500rpm. Bordino engaged Antonio Ascari's Alfa Romeo P2 in a furious duel that wrecked his brakes at halfway. Fiat withdrew from racing after this event but supported renewed efforts by its fastest driver in America, where Bordino had won races in 1922 with a modified Fiat 802. By then, however, Duesenberg and Miller were too good for Bordino's single-seater version of the 805. Apart from a brief comeback at Monza in 1927 with its complex, 185bhp 806 (with two blown six-cylinder engines in tandem), Fiat never raced again.

ABOVE: Louis Zborowski leads Sunbeam's Kenelm Lee Guinness between the rudimentary fences at Lyons in 1924, his white, ex-works Miller 122 displaying its American board track heritage. Miller entered three of these new 2-liter cars (with hemispherical-topped combustion chambers) for the Italian and Spanish Grands Prix in 1923, when Jimmy Murphy finished third at Monza, and Zborowski was robbed of victory at Sitges by a burst tire. Zborowski bought one of the cars and raced it at Lyons as the first private entrant ever to contest a Grand Prix. Ten weeks later, he was killed at Monza while driving one of four straight-eight Mercedes in their only Grand Prix appearance.

OPPOSITE: Kenelm Lee Guinness shoots the hairpin at Les Sept Chemins, at the northern extreme of the Circuit de Lyons, during his duel in 1924 with Giuseppe Campari, who has lined up his Alfa Romeo P2 on the widest possible line into the corner. The Sunbeam was halted by an engine failure, and Campari went on to win. Guinness, the founder of the KLG sparkplug manufacturer, won voiturette races for STD but never a Grand Prix. Three weeks after Dario Resta's death, he had a career-ending crash that killed riding mechanic Bill Perkins in the San Sebastian Grand Prix, which was won by his teammate, Henry Segrave.

ABOVE LEFT: Vittorio Jano's 135mph Alfa Romeo 8C-2000 P2, its blown straight-eight developing 140bhp at 5500rpm, won on debut at Lyons in 1924 with Campari. This was a terrific race, led in turn by the Sunbeams of Henry Segrave and Kenelm Lee Guinness, Pietro Bordino's Fiat, and Antonio Ascari's P2, which was in front with 2 laps to go when overheating cracked its cylinder head. Here riding mechanic Giulio Ramponi vainly tries to push-start the stricken car. Uprated to 155bhp, the P2 won the inaugural AIACR Manufacturers championship in 1925, when Ascari's death at Montlhéry was a factor in Alfa Romeo's decision to follow Fiat out of Grand Prix racing.

ABOVE RIGHT: Bugatti overcame Delage to win the very poorly supported AIACR Manufacturers title in 1926, the first season of the new 1.5-liter formula, for which it built the supercharged type 39A. Bugatti fielded a powerful works team of these 130bhp cars, led by Meo Costantini, Jules Goux, Emilio Materassi, and Ferdinando Minoia. Goux won an absurd Grand Prix de l'ACF on the Miramas speedway in southern France—a race contested only by three Bugattis—and a seven-car Grand Prix of Europe at Lasarte, Spain. This is Costantini refueling his 39A at Lasarte before resuming to finish third, behind a Delage raced by Edmond Bourlier/Robert Sénéchal.

ABOVE: All the drivers of the new Delage 15-S8 had to endure overheating throughout 1926, due to the proximity of the exhaust pipe to a cramped cockpit, and it was so severe that they suffered blisters on their right legs and feet. The team had to use replacement drivers in all the races. Nevertheless, in the absence of the works Bugatti team, Delage contrived to win the inaugural RAC Grand Prix at Brooklands, which was contested by nine cars. The winning 15-S8 was raced by Robert Sénéchal (at center, holding his cap) until he was relieved by Louis Wagner. Their teammates, Robert Benoist and André Dubonnet, came in third of three finishers.

OPPOSITE: Sandbanks were installed on the bland concrete expanse of the Brooklands speedway for the inaugural RAC Grand Prix in 1926. Bugatti did not send its works team, but a 1-2 by Delage was prevented by Malcolm Campbell with his newly acquired Bugatti 39A. Here Campbell leads Albert Divo, debuting the fast but fragile new 1.5-liter Talbot 700, around one of these artificial chicanes. Brooklands was to have staged a Grand Prix the previous year, but it had been canceled due to local objections to noise pollution. For this race, all the cars were required to be fitted with silencers to avoid disruption to the suburban gentility of nearby Weybridge.

ABOVE LEFT: "Williams" (the racing pseudonym of William Grover-Williams) speeds past the grandstands of the Montlhéry speedway in 1927 in his blown straight-eight Talbot 700. STD's voiturette racing team was so successful that the cars and drivers became popularly known as the Invincibles, but these were now lean times for the company in Grand Prix racing. Teamed here with Albert Divo and Louis Wagner, Williams was the only Talbot driver to be classified as a finisher, fourth behind three Delages. Engine failures accounted for both his teammates, and Wagner—the last active driver to have raced in the first Grand Prix 21 years before—finally retired after this event.

ABOVE RIGHT: When the Delage 15-S8 replaced the successful V12 2LCV in 1926, its twin-supercharged, 1.5-liter straight-eight delivered 165bhp to a five-speed gearbox at an unprecedented 8400rpm. The car's performance was compromised by cockpit overheating throughout the season, so it was substantially modified for 1927. This potent engine was fitted with a single supercharger and mounted off-center to move the propshaft to the left, creating more space for the driver, and the exhaust pipe was also relocated to the left side. Here is Edmond Bourlier driving the modified car into second place in the 1927 Grand Prix de l'ACF at Montlhéry behind his team leader, Robert Benoist.

ABOVE: French wartime fighter pilot Robert Benoist warmed up for the 1927 season by winning a nonchampionship race at Montlhéry, and went on to dominate all four Grands Prix in the AIACR Manufacturers championship, in Paris again, and then at Lasarte, Monza, and Brooklands. He is pictured after heading Edmond Bourlier and Albert Divo in a Delage 1-2-3 in the season-closing RAC Grand Prix, leaving the works Bugattis of Louis Chiron and Emilio Materassi far behind. A beaming Robert Sénéchal, acting as the team's reserve driver this day, is holding the flowers. Louis Delage dissolved his team after this outstanding season, but the cars were sold and raced on as voiturettes.

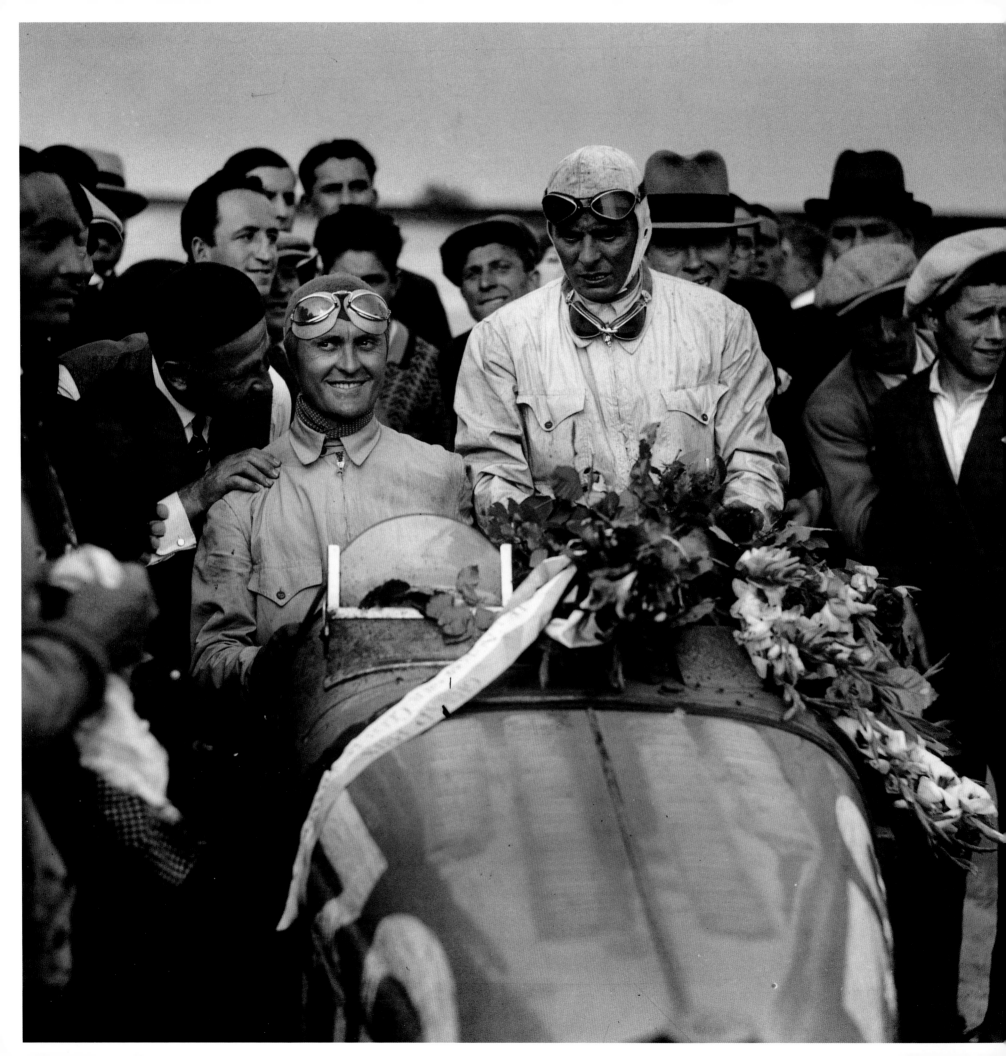

CHAPTER 3

Free Spirits
1928–1933

T he new AIACR Grand Prix formula for 1928 derestricted engine swept volume but stopped just short of Formule Libre. In the midst of a grim and worsening world financial crisis, no new cars were built specifically to comply with the AIACR rules. And, apart from the usual approximate interpretation by the AAA, only the Italian Grand Prix formally catered to them.

The race at Monza actually had an entry of 22 cars, and a crowd of 120,000. It was won by Louis Chiron's Bugatti 35 from Achille Varzi's Alfa Romeo P2 and another Bugatti driven by Tazio Nuvolari— three young men embarking on spectacular careers. It was also the occasion of the worst accident in Grand Prix history, involving one of several 1.5-liter Talbots that had passed into Italian ownership when STD pulled out of racing at the end of 1927. Successful former Bugatti and Itala driver Emilio Materassi suffered a steering failure and hurtled over a ditch and into a grandstand. He died, and so did 22 spectators.

The promoters of the other major races used the Formule Libre format, and the ACF went so far as to run its Grand Prix as a handicap race for sports cars. The AIACR annulled its World Championship of Manufacturers, and would do so again in both 1929 and 1930.

The AIACR tried an ill-conceived fuel formula in 1929, to which only the French and Spanish Grand Prix organizers catered, and a minimum weight formula in 1930, which was used only for the Belgian Grand Prix. Then it came up with complex regulations for 1931, based on a sliding scale of minimum weights set against the swept volumes of naturally aspirated engines up to 5000cc. The promoters and teams ignored them. The AIACR effectively gave up and restricted itself merely to stipulating the minimum race lengths. It first tried a long-distance format before reducing the distances toward a length that is familiar today.

OPPOSITE: Louis Chiron looks happier than a clearly exhausted Achille Varzi after their 4-lap victory together in the 10-hour Grand Prix on the Montlhéry in 1931. The winning average speed of their works-entered, 2-liter, 160bhp Bugatti 51 was 79mph, including pit stops. With Tazio Nuvolari, these were the outstanding professional drivers of the Formule Libre period. All three were in demand from the top teams throughout the era and won races for both Alfa Romeo and Bugatti, while Nuvolari and Varzi also won for Maserati. Including the shared drives, Chiron and Nuvolari each secured 19 victories in major races between 1928 and 1933, Varzi 16.

Great Depression there certainly was, but motor races were plentiful, although there were relatively few in which the leading teams and drivers met face to face. Mercedes-Benz participated effectively on occasion with stripped-down sports cars, as did Bentley, but the foremost manufacturers in the Formule Libre seasons were Bugatti and its Italian rivals, Alfa Romeo and Maserati. All three produced Formule Libre "specials."

Maserati, which had made its Grand Prix debut at Monza in 1926 with two supercharged 1500cc straight-eight cars, introduced the outrageous, 150mph 16C-4000 V4, powered by two 2-liter straight-eights mounted side-by-side, each with its own supercharger. The "Sedici Cilindri" Maserati set a Monza lap record in 1929 at 124.2mph, a speed unsurpassed on the Autodromo until 1954, and was formidable the following season in the hands of Baconin Borzacchini, who also raced it (without its blowers) at Indy.

Both Alfa Romeo and Bugatti responded in 1931. Vittorio Jano's special, with two 1750cc straight-sixes mounted side-by-side to provide more than 260bhp, was the unwieldy, 160mph Alfa Romeo Tipo A, which killed Luigi Arcangeli during practice at Monza. Ettore Bugatti, ever the purist, declined to go the twin-engine route but produced the type 54, powered by a blown 4.9-liter straight-eight also producing more than 260bhp.

The Maserati and the Bugatti each had two victories in big races, the Alfa Romeo only one, and on the whole the winning was done by more conventional cars.

It was Alfa Romeo that succeeded in both the AIACR's first European Championships of Drivers, securing the top three positions each year. In 1931, when only the organizers of the Italian, French, and Belgian Grands Prix complied with the grueling 10-hour, two-driver rule, Ferdinando Minoia won the title without winning a race, narrowly outscoring Giuseppe Campari and Borzacchini. Nuvolari beat Borzacchini and Rudi Caracciola to the 1932 championship, which was based on the Italian, French, and German Grands Prix.

Alfa Romeo left motor racing on this exceptional high, entrusting its cars entirely to the Scuderia Ferrari for the 1933 season, in which, despite incursions by Varzi for Bugatti and Nuvolari for Maserati, Chiron and Luigi Fagioli were very strong.

Alfa Romeo would not be flying high for long.

GRAND PRIX REGULATIONS

1928 *AIACR Grand Prix formula. Engines: free. Dry weight: 550kg (1323lb) minimum, 750kg (1653lb) maximum. Race distance: 600km (372 miles) minimum.* **1929–30** *AIACR Grand Prix formula. Engines: free. Dry weight: 900kg (1980lb) minimum, plus 14kg (31lb) of oil and commercially available fuel, no replenishment within a distance of 100km (62 miles). Body width: 1000mm minimum.* **1930** *Engine piston displacement: 1100cc minimum. Fuel: benzol additive 30% maximum.* **1931–33** *Formule Libre. AIACR race duration: 10 hours minimum, two drivers.* **1932** *AIACR race duration: 5 hours minimum, 10 hours maximum.* **1933** *AIACR race distance: 500km (310 miles) minimum.*

AIACR EUROPEAN CHAMPIONSHIP OF DRIVERS

1931	*Ferdinando Minoia*	*Alfa Romeo*
1932	*Tazio Nuvolari*	*Alfa Romeo*

ABOVE LEFT: New supercharged versions of the straight-eight Bugatti 35 set the standard early in the Formule Libre period. Here William Grover-Williams, driving the solo works-tended 2.3-liter 35B, negotiates the narrow Portier corner during the inaugural Monaco Grand Prix in April 1929. His passing is closely observed by chefs starting a tradition of leaving the kitchens of the principality's many hotels and restaurants to watch racing cars in this confined environment. Williams won after a famously unlikely race-leading performance by Rudi Caracciola's massive Mercedes SSK. Bugatti's other Formule Libre winners included Louis Chiron, Tazio Nuvolari, and Achille Varzi, as well as René Dreyfus and Marcel Lehoux.

ABOVE RIGHT: Maserati produced the very effective, blown 2.5-liter 8C-2500 26M in 1931, when Luigi Fagioli and Achille Varzi used its 185bhp and exceptional handling to win five of the major races, humbling even the Alfa Romeo, Bugatti, and Maserati specials. Clemente Biondetti and Luigi Parenti shared third place in the 1931 Grand Prix de l'ACF at the wheel of this 26M, pictured leading the aging Delage 15-S8 of Robert Sénéchal, who finished fifth without a codriver. The 1933 version of the Maserati 26M had a 2.9-liter, 205bhp engine and hydraulic braking all around, and Tazio Nuvolari raced it to several victories at the expense of Scuderia Ferrari's Alfa Romeos.

OPPOSITE: A mixed field of 23 Formule Libre cars built by Alfa Romeo, Bugatti, Delage, Maserati, Mercedes-Benz, and Sunbeam take the start of the 1931 Grand Prix de l'ACF on the concrete speedway at Montlhéry. This was the second of three races run that season to the AIACR's 10-hour format. In the foreground is the No. 18 Alfa Romeo Monza of Giuseppe Campari, which, with Baconin Borzacchini codriving, finished in second place. The winning car was the Bugatti 51 of Louis Chiron and Achille Varzi (at top left, beyond the white Mercedes SSK raced by Rudi Caracciola and Otto Merz). Maseratis were third and fourth.

ABOVE: Baconin Borzacchini (left) and Giuseppe Campari stand together in their Alfa Romeo Monza after finishing second in the 10-hour contest at Montlhéry. Two years later, Campari returned to the Paris speedway to win the Grand Prix de l'ACF with a Maserati 8C-3000. It was his last victory. On a black day for motor racing at Monza later in 1933, both these drivers lost their lives when Campari's Alfa Romeo spun and was hit by Borzacchini's works Maserati. It was to have been the swan-song race before a richly earned retirement for the popular Campari, who had scored his and Alfa Romeo's first big win at Mugello back in 1920.

OPPOSITE: With the grid formed, a drivers' briefing is in progress on a rainy July day in the Eifel Mountains in 1931. The first three German Grands Prix on the magnificent new Nürburgring had been sports car races, all won by Mercedes-Benz, and this was the first for Formule Libre race cars. At the end of the race, however, the outstanding three drivers of the period were soundly beaten. Rudi Caracciola won the 500km race with a stripped Mercedes SSKL, defeating Louis Chiron and Achille Varzi in Bugatti 51s and Tazio Nuvolari in an Alfa Romeo Monza. Other SSKLs, driven by Otto Merz and Hans Stuck, completed the top six.

ABOVE: Rudi Caracciola winds up his Mercedes-Benz SSKL toward its 150mph top speed during his winning drive in the rainy 1931 German Grand Prix. The latest 7.1-liter version of the supercharged straight-six, designed in 1926 by Ferdinand Porsche, developed over 300bhp. Mercedes withdrew at the end of this season, and Caracciola switched to Alfa Romeo, driving P3s to two victories in 1932. He then formed his own team but broke a leg at Monaco in April 1933, and he was unable to race until Mercedes ran him at Montlhéry in July 1934. Even with one leg shorter than the other, he began establishing his reputation as one of the finest drivers of all time.

BELOW: The start of the 1933 Nice Grand Prix, on the seafront of the popular Côte d'Azur resort, was given by guest of honor Felice Nazzaro, and the race was contested by many of the best-known drivers of the day. The Monza Alfa Romeos of two prodigiously talented young drivers, Jean-Pierre Wimille and Guy Moll, are at the front of the pack, ahead of Marcel Lehoux's privately entered Bugatti 51, Achille Varzi's works 51, Tazio Nuvolari's race-winning Maserati 8CM, Giuseppe Campari's Maserati 4CM, René Dreyfus's works Bugatti, and the Alfa Romeos of Raymond Sommer and Luigi Fagioli, the latter on debut with Scuderia Ferrari.

CHAPTER 4

Silver Arrows
1934–1939

During 1932, the AIACR resolved to devise regulations with the dual purpose of uniting the big Formule Libre races and bringing performance and costs under control. In October that year, it announced a new Grand Prix formula for 1934 that placed no restrictions on engine swept volume or fuel, but was based on a maximum dry weight of 750kg. The AIACR committed itself to this concept for three seasons.

The new regulations were catered to the midrange Libre cars that existed at the end of the 1932 season, such as the 2.6-liter Alfa Romeo, the 2.3-liter Bugatti, and the 3-liter Maserati, because the AIACR reckoned that these cars would deliver the desired level of performance. With 200bhp supercharged engines and top speeds of about 140mph, they had been inferior to specials like the Alfa Romeo Tipo A, the Bugatti 54, and the Maserati V4—not to mention a monstrous Mercedes-Benz SSKL "streamliner" with which the relatively unknown Manfred von Brauchitsch had defeated everyone on the AVUS in 1932. When Otto Merz was killed in a similar, works-entered SSKL on the very fast Berlin track in 1933, it seemed to justify the AIACR's decision.

That decision remains, however, the most misguided one ever reached by a motor sport sanctioning body. The AIACR assumed that development would remain static, grossly underestimating the effects of new technology, notably lightweight metals. The 750kg formula led directly to the most technically advanced, the most expensive, and the fastest racing cars that had ever existed, with power outputs that would not be surpassed for 50 years. The formula was extended into a fourth season in 1937, and the potency of the front-running cars was hardly reduced by the AIACR's replacement formula in 1938. Their maximum speeds had risen to 190mph in 1937 and, equipped with two-stage supercharging, they

OPPOSITE: Hans Stuck wrestled his Auto Union Typ A into a narrow lead of the 1934 Grand Prix de l'ACF, but the effort ruined his tires and he was in the Montlhéry pits early. Stuck rejoined and stayed in the race longer than teammate Auguste Momberger and all three Mercedes-Benz drivers, but his P-Wagen could not mount a challenge to the winning Alfa Romeo P3, a 2-year-old design. Stuck's run was finally halted by a water pump failure 8 laps before the finish. The new German racing effort looked ineffectual here, but the Silver Arrows would never have to endure such humiliation again.

were capable of 185mph in 1939.

As envisioned, there was no shortage of cars from Alfa Romeo, Bugatti, and Maserati, and these companies initially set out to modify existing designs. An unprecedented 25 races were arranged for cars complying with the new formula and, at first, Scuderia Ferrari was successful after fitting a bigger engine to the Alfa Romeo P3. But Auto Union and Mercedes-Benz carefully studied the new rules and, with Nazi funding, had sufficient notice to design immensely powerful cars, with aerodynamically efficient bodies enclosing their radiators, that would change Grand Prix racing forever.

The funding from the Third Reich is estimated to have made up only about 20% of the budgets of the two German teams. Nevertheless, they regularly decimated the Italian opposition after the second season of the 750kg formula. In 1936, Maserati produced the first-ever Grand Prix car with a V8, but its supercharged 4.8-liter motor developed 320bhp at 5300rpm—no match for the Silver Arrows. Alfa Romeo, which had some Italian state funding, had the spirit to mount a consistent if rarely successful resistance and, in 1937, took its operation back in-house, firing Vittorio Jano but retaining Enzo Ferrari as its team manager. Yet Gioachino Colombo's new 8C-308 was not the answer, and nor were experimental V12 and V16 projects. After Tazio Nuvolari's 308 caught fire at Pau, Alfa Romeo lost its fastest driver to Auto Union and subsequently joined Maserati in voiturette racing.

Mercedes-Benz held the upper hand except in 1936, when its inferior chassis was outperformed by the Auto Union. Powered by engines producing as much as 650bhp, transmitted to the track surface through such narrow tires, these cars were immensely difficult to handle. The few who managed to master them were nothing less than heroic. Ten of Auto Union's 23 victories were scored by Bernd Rosemeyer, 4 by Hans Stuck, and 3 each by Achille Varzi and Nuvolari. No fewer than 16 of 33 wins by Mercedes were achieved by Rudi Caracciola, 9 by Hermann Lang, and 5 by Luigi Fagioli. The AIACR's European Championship of Drivers, each based on a selection of the big races, was a German benefit, of course.

Maserati's fast but fragile 8CTF project for the 3-liter formula in 1938 was a token effort (although one car was sold to American Wilbur Shaw and won the Indy 500 in both 1939 and 1940). By 1939, Auto Union and Mercedes were effectively unopposed. These exceptional Grand Prix teams contested their last race in Belgrade, Yugoslavia, a few hours after World War II was declared on September 3.

GRAND PRIX REGULATIONS

1934–37 *AIACR Grand Prix formula. Engines: free. Dry weight: 750kg (1653lb) maximum. Bodywork cross-section: 850x250mm minimum at cockpit. Race distance: 500km minimum.* **1938–39** *AIACR Grand Prix formula. Engine piston displacement: 1000cc minimum, 4500cc maximum (naturally aspirated), 666cc minimum, 3000cc maximum (forced induction). Dry weight: 400kg (882lb) minimum, 850kg (1874lb) maximum, defined on sliding scale according to engine piston displacement and including wheels and tires. Bodywork width: 850mm minimum.*

AIACR EUROPEAN CHAMPIONSHIP OF DRIVERS

1935	Rudi Caracciola	Mercedes-Benz
1936	Bernd Rosemeyer	Auto Union
1937	Rudi Caracciola	Mercedes-Benz
1938	Rudi Caracciola	Mercedes-Benz
1939	Hermann Müller	Auto Union*

The 1939 title was never officially awarded by the AIACR.

ABOVE: Tazio Nuvolari finished fifth in the 1934 Monaco Grand Prix, the first race under the 750kg formula, with the 2.9-liter straight-eight Bugatti 59. An evolution of a model introduced at the 1933 Spanish Grand Prix, a 59 won the Grand Prix at Spa later in the season in the hands of René Dreyfus—after the German teams had withdrawn their entries, refusing to pay Belgian import duty on their alcohol-based fuel. Jean-Pierre Wimille and Maurice Trintignant also won minor races with the Bugatti 59, which was equipped with a 3.3-liter, 260bhp engine in 1935 and later a 4.7-liter version of Bugatti's sports car engine.

ABOVE: Scuderia Ferrari upgraded the P3 in 1934–35 with independent front suspension and a 3.2-liter, 270bhp version of Alfa Romeo's straight-eight. Guy Moll followed up a Monaco victory with another in the 1934 Formule Libre race on the AVUS with this curiosity, a streamlined version that added nothing to the P3's purposeful looks. Mercedes-Benz did not race in the Avusrennen, but Auto Union made its debut although it encountered mechanical problems. However, Moll still had to overcome Achille Varzi in a conventional P3. His promise was not fulfilled; a brief, meteoric career ended when he was killed at Pescara during another major Libre race, the Coppa Acerbo, later in the season.

OPPOSITE: A nonchalant Hans Stuck stands by in the paddock at Montlhéry in July 1934, perhaps aware that the technical innovations of his P-Wagen Auto Union Typ A may not be fully appreciated by everyone in the group gathered around it. The car was based on a torsionally stiff chassis (the first tubular frame) and—another first—torsion-bar independent suspension of all four wheels. But the biggest innovation was its engine location. The design team had included engineers who had been involved in the short-lived, mid-engined Benz RH project back in 1923. They had urged project leader Ferdinand Porsche to locate the supercharged, 4.4-liter, 32-valve, 295bhp V16 behind the driver.

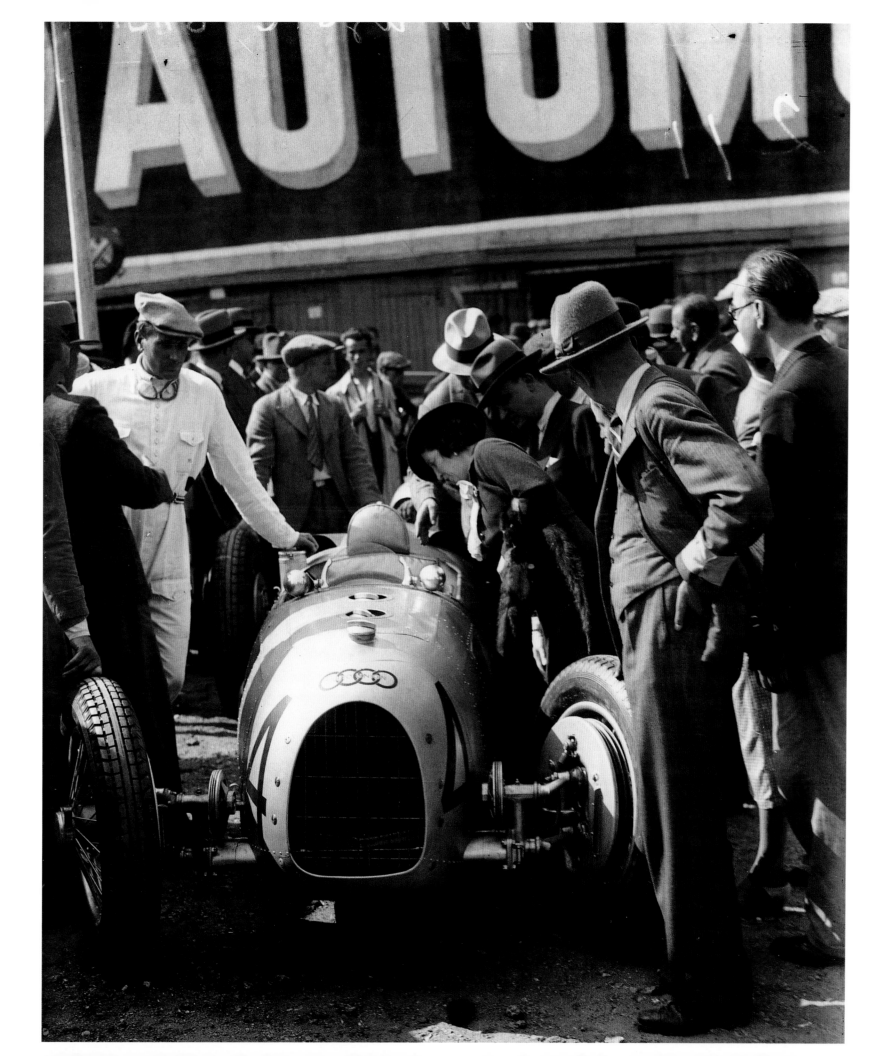

OPPOSITE: Grid positions for the 1934 Grand Prix de l'ACF were drawn by ballot, and Louis Chiron started on the third row. He made a dream start, lunging his Alfa Romeo P3 ahead of Rudi Caracciola's Mercedes-Benz W25, Achille Varzi's P3, René Dreyfus's Bugatti 59, Hans Stuck's Auto Union Typ A, and Tazio Nuvolari's Bugatti. After an early struggle with Stuck, Chiron had the measure of the new German cars in this 500km race on the full Montlhéry course even before, one by one, they were all stopped by mechanical problems. A 1-2-3 for Scuderia Ferrari was completed by Varzi and Guy Moll, who took over Felice Trossi's P3 at halfway.

ABOVE LEFT: The big Parisian crowd at the Montlhéry *autodrome* in 1934 watched Bugatti comprehensively outperformed by Alfa Romeo, Auto Union, and Mercedes-Benz, but Robert Benoist's 59 finished fourth—and last. Here two of the new Mercedes head down the finish straight as Hans Stuck's Auto Union leaves the pits. This was also the first Grand Prix for the Mercedes W25, which had had a winning debut with Manfred von Brauchitsch on the Nürburgring in the Eifelrennen Formule Libre race. It was an inauspicious start; all were out after only 15 of the 40 laps. A fortnight later, the Alfa Romeos were also-rans in the German Grand Prix on the Nürburgring.

ABOVE RIGHT: Tazio Nuvolari's 1935 Nürburgring victory was probably his greatest. Soon after the start—the first signaled by lights, red-amber-green—Nuvolari spun his 3.8-liter Alfa Romeo P3, and later Scuderia Ferrari's pressure hose failed and the car had to be refueled from churns. Yet Nuvolari's inspired recovery put the leader, Manfred von Brauchitsch, under such pressure that a tire of his Mercedes blew on the last lap. Nuvolari came through to win with eight German cars behind him and a big posse of Nazi officials in the VIP stand. The organizers had not bothered to bring any national anthem but Germany's. Nuvolari politely handed them a recording of Italy's anthem from his briefcase.

ABOVE: The English aristocrat and the German superstar. The Viscount Curzon, Francis Richard Henry Penn, aka. Earl Howe, links arms with Rudi Caracciola on the grid at Donington in 1937. Two years after Howe took up racing at the age of 44 in 1928, he bought a Mercedes-Benz SSK that "Caratsch" had raced. He was a consistent competitor with various Alfa Romeo, Bugatti, Delage, and MG cars and was now a member of the works ERA team and the president of the British Racing Drivers' Club. Caracciola, en route to the second of his three AIACR European titles, is set to finish third with his Mercedes W125, lapping Howe three times.

OPPOSITE: The Mercedes-Benz team cars stand gleamingly ready to receive (left to right) Rudi Caracciola, Manfred von Brauchitsch, and Luigi Fagioli before the 1935 Grand Prix de l'ACF at Montlhéry. The W25 with which the company entered the 750kg formula had all-independent suspension, the first integral gearbox/differential assembly, and a supercharged, 3.4-liter straight-eight engine producing almost 360bhp. For this season, a 4-liter iteration of the engine delivered 445bhp through the first limited-slip differential. The W25Bs finished this race first, second, and fourth in the above order, the interloper being Goffredo Zehender's Maserati 6C-34, an interim car that was raced before the arrival of the disappointing V8-RI.

OPPOSITE: The British crowd waiting for their first sight of the Silver Arrows in the 1937 Donington Grand Prix were able to place bets at the venue. The bookies had never seen the German cars, either, and made ERA driver Arthur Dobson their prerace favorite. Enthralled by the sight of Auto Union and Mercedes-Benz swamping the first five positions, the crowd failed to notice the bookies quietly packing up their gear and doing a runner. Punters who had wagered on Bernd Rosemeyer included his mechanics. The race organizers had the grace to honor their bets, and they were not the ones who enthusiastically set fire to the bookies' hastily abandoned wooden stands.

ABOVE: The Mercedes-Benz team manager, Alfred Neubauer, signals to Manfred von Brauchitsch that a pit stop is due at Donington Park in 1937. The rotund former works driver was now in charge of up to 100 race team mechanics and the deployment of as many as eight chassis, which were used in rotation. Neubauer was the first team manager to use pit boards to keep the drivers informed (at Solitude in 1926) and established many new procedures that set the standards for today's highly professional approach—not to mention tricks such as foxing the opposition with enigmatic signals that only he and his drivers understood.

ABOVE: Alfred Neubauer looks on as Manfred von Brauchitsch's Mercedes-Benz W125 undergoes a tire change before finishing second in the 1937 Donington Grand Prix. Mercedes went up a blind alley in 1936, installing a 4.7-liter iteration of the straight-eight, delivering 495bhp through a transverse gearbox, in a short-wheelbase chassis. But the new W125, with a 5.7-liter engine producing almost 650bhp, set new standards not only in power but also in roadholding, with the first front suspension using double wishbones and coil springs (with hydraulic instead of friction-type dampers), and the first racing application of a De Dion tube at the rear. The W125 swept all before it.

OPPOSITE: Bernd Rosemeyer takes the checkered flag to win the Donington Grand Prix in 1937. Auto Union had increased the swept volume of its V16 to 5 liters in 1935, boosting its output to 375bhp, but the five-speed Typ C raced in 1936–37 with 6 liters and upward of 520bhp. This car brought Auto Union and Rosemeyer their most successful season in 1936, but usually failed to match the Mercedes W125 in the last year of the 750kg formula, although Rosemeyer won the Eifelrennen, Coppa Acerbo, and Vanderbilt Cup. This was his final major victory. He was killed fewer than 4 months later during a record attempt on a German autobahn.

ABOVE: Jean-Pierre Wimille's great talent was insufficient to overcome the shortcomings at Bugatti, and he qualified at the back of a nine-car starting grid at Reims in 1938, more than 20 seconds off the front-running pace of the latest Mercedes. For the new formula, Bugatti built two reduced versions of its 4.7-liter straight-eight, a naturally aspirated 4.5-liter and a blown 3-liter, and fitted them into rebodied type 59 chassis. This is the supercharged 59/50B, which, probably to the relief of the driver and his mechanics, has just burst an oil line on the first lap. After committing this expenditure, Bugatti retreated to voiturette and sports car racing.

OPPOSITE: Richard Seaman stands in the Mercedes-Benz pit at Reims during the 1938 Grand Prix de l'ACF. The 6-foot, 3-inch Englishman was signed on a contract personally approved by Adolf Hitler as a junior driver in 1937. He was retained for 1938 but used as the reserve driver. Three weeks after Reims, Seaman raced for the first time in 9 months when seven cars were sent to the Nürburgring and, to the great embarrassment of the assembled Nazi hierarchy, he won the German Grand Prix. Seaman lost his life when he was leading again at Spa in 1939; the crash broke his right arm and knocked him unconscious, and his W154 caught fire.

OPPOSITE: In preparing for the new AIACR formula in 1938, Mercedes-Benz secured the consultancy services of Ferdinand Porsche, who recommended a naturally aspirated 4.5-liter V12. Like Auto Union, however, Mercedes eventually opted for a blown 3-liter V12, which was mounted at an angle in the W154 chassis and drove through the company's first five-speed gearbox. This is the business end of Hermann Lang's car at Reims, where he was entrusted with the most powerful engine produced that season. It developed a tad under 475bhp at 8000rpm on a "boost" pressure of 1.44bar, and Lang put it on pole position at just under 110mph.

ABOVE: All alone in his work, flat in fifth, high on speed, Hermann Lang hurtles down one of the long straightaways between the huge fields bordering the Reims-Gueux circuit, having long been traveling at 175mph. Lang's low-line Mercedes-Benz W154 was delayed in the 1938 Grand Prix de l'ACF when the engine was slow to restart after a pit stop. It was Manfred von Brauchitsch who led the Mercedes 1-2-3 from Rudi Caracciola, with Lang a lap down. That season the W154 won six victories in major events, and the evolutionary 1939 car, which was raced regularly with 480bhp and could hit 185mph on this track, added four more.

ABOVE: Korpsführer Adolf Hühnlein (far right) struts his stuff before the 1938 German Grand Prix on the Nürburgring, talking with (left to right) current drivers Rudi Caracciola and Manfred von Brauchitsch, and former drivers Max Sailer and Alfred Neubauer, now team executives. Appointed by Adolf Hitler to oversee how his Reichmarks were spent, Hühnlein was a regular figure on the Grand Prix scene from 1934. Most of the Silver Arrows personnel saw Hühnlein as a humorless bully and were mightily relieved that he possessed insufficient technical knowledge to interfere in the operation of the teams. At the end of this race meeting, it fell to him to tell Hitler that an Englishman had won.

OPPOSITE: René Dreyfus drops his sports car–derived Delahaye 145 into the Karussel on the Nürburgring during his drive into fifth place in the 1938 German Grand Prix. The naturally aspirated 4.5-liter solution was adopted for the 1938–39 formula by French companies Delahaye and Talbot. Dreyfus had begun Delahaye's program with a nonstop strategy that yielded a remarkable victory in the nonchampionship Pau Grand Prix (to which Mercedes-Benz and Alfa Romeo sent teams), and by winning again against lesser opposition a fortnight later in Cork, Ireland. This bulky car was replaced in 1939 by the purpose-built V12 Delahaye 155, but it was not competitive.

OPPOSITE: Two of the four races in the 1939 AIACR championship fell to Hermann Lang's Mercedes-Benz W163, one to Hermann Müller's Auto Union Typ D, and one to Rudi Caracciola's Mercedes. Lang was declared the champion at the expense of Müller, the rightful winner because his other qualifying results were superior. Lang started out with Mercedes as Luigi Fagioli's chief mechanic in 1934, and he was regarded with disdain by some of his colleagues, especially the aristocratic Manfred von Brauchitsch. He is pictured in pit lane with his wife, Lydia (right), and Alice "Baby" Caracciola. Lang's speed in 1939 certainly merited his title, also taking him to two nonchampionship victories.

ABOVE: The Auto Union Typ D for the new formula in 1938–39 was equipped with a blown 3-liter V12 developing more than 480bhp, fed from lateral sidepod fuel cells that gave the car a much more attractive appearance. The team's three cars were opposed by four Mercedes at Monza in 1938, and Tazio Nuvolari could qualify only fifth, but the W154s encountered a series of engine-related failures. To the undisguised delight of the Italian crowd, Nuvolari threaded his way through the trees to take the win. His young compatriot, Giuseppe Farina, finished second with a works Alfa Romeo 316, an eccentric Gioachino Colombo design powered by two 175bhp straight-eights.

ABOVE: Hermann Müller is introduced by Dick Seaman to the Duke of Kent on the starting grid of the 1938 Donington Grand Prix. Müller, whose Auto Union finished fourth in the race, became the subject of a controversy the following season that is unresolved to this day. The outbreak of World War II caused the cancelation of the Italian Grand Prix and the AIACR to cease its activities before declaring the winner of its 1939 European championship. Under the presumed points system, Müller should have been awarded the title, but Mercedes-Benz persuaded Korpsführer Hühnlein's NSKK (National Socialist Motoring Corps) retrospectively and unilaterally to declare Hermann Lang the champion.

OPPOSITE: The German teams arrived at Donington Park for the 1938 race just as the Munich crisis unfolded, and they were ordered to leave England immediately by the German embassy in London. The mechanics packed up the trucks and left for the ferry at Harwich with orders to set fire to the cars if stopped on the road. When the immediate threat of war was averted, the race was rescheduled, and the Silver Arrows returned 3 weeks later. Here Hermann Müller's Auto Union vainly defends third place from Richard Seaman's Mercedes-Benz at the Old Hairpin late in the race. Their respective teammates, Tazio Nuvolari and Hermann Lang, finished first and second.

ABOVE: What a star he was! Tazio Nuvolari, the popular (non-German) victor of the delayed 1938 Donington Grand Prix, shows his very broadest grin after wowing the crowd with his car control. Recovering his composure after his Auto Union had struck and killed a stag during practice, Nuvolari survived a big moment on spilled oil that put him on the grass, hurled his car at the corners to catch up, broke the lap record repeatedly, and won after Hermann Lang was hampered by a broken windshield on his Mercedes. The next driver to win a Grand Prix on this track also possessed amazing car control and charisma: Ayrton Senna, 55 years later.

OPPOSITE: The Typ D Auto Unions of Tazio Nuvolari and Hermann Müller lead off the line in the 1939 Grand Prix at Reims. Nuvolari soon lost the lead to Hermann Lang's Mercedes-Benz, and then his gearbox broke, leaving Lang unchallenged. Team manager Alfred Neubauer signaled him to ease up, but his V12 inexplicably broke a piston at two-thirds distance. With the other Mercedes already gone, Müller drove on to secure the only Grand Prix victory of his career in a team 1-2 with the courageous Georg Meier, painfully a lap behind after badly burning an arm when spilled fuel ignited in a pit stop.

CHAPTER 5

Forza Alfa Romeo!
1946–1951

The industrial might of Germany was again decimated by World War II, which left the racing companies in France and Italy in similar, if less parlous, situations. What European automobile industry remained had other priorities, but it was not long before race promoters began the process of reviving Grand Prix racing.

The international governing body—the former AIACR—was reformed, renamed the Federation Internationale de l'Automobile (FIA), and convened in February 1946, seven months after VE Day, to create a new Grand Prix formula. By necessity, the FIA based Formula A on the cars that had survived the war. A number of 1.5-liter voiturettes had been hidden away during the hostilities—straight-eight Alfa Romeos and straight-four Maseratis in Italy, and straight-six ERAs in Britain. There were also Grand Prix Delahayes and Talbots in France, the naturally aspirated ("atmospheric") 4.5-liter engines of which had been unable to match the performance of the supercharged Silver Arrows of the 1938–39 seasons. It was decided that a formula should be workable if it accommodated them and the blown 1500s.

The FIA also created Formula B for naturally aspirated, 2-liter voiturettes, and Formula C for small single-seaters with midmounted 500cc motorcycle engines, which were now being built and raced in increasing numbers by European amateurs. The new categories came into effect in 1948 and were renamed 1, 2, and 3 in 1949.

In the meantime, almost 20 well-supported Formule Libre races were run in 1946, and the 1947 season began with the new *Temporada* (Spanish for "season") of Libre races in South America, before the Swiss, Belgian, Italian, and French (ACF) Grands Prix were revived in the European summer. Two years later, after a World Championship had been established in motorcycle racing, the FIA recognized

---

OPPOSITE: The Alfa Romeo 158s of Juan Fangio and Reg Parnell (in white coveralls) are fettled on the Silverstone grid before the 1950 Grand Prix of Europe, sharing the front row with their two sister cars. The first pole position in the new World Championship was occupied by Antonio "Nino" Farina, with Luigi Fagioli second. Alfa Corse had been undefeated since the war and, under chief engineer Orazio Satta Puliga, had quietly continued development of its race car during 1949. With a World Championship on offer, the outstanding team of the era returned with a 360bhp iteration of its supercharged straight-eight, and maintained its unbeaten record until 1951.

that the time was right to create one for Formula 1 drivers. The European races selected for inclusion were the British, Monaco, Swiss, Belgian, French, and Italian Grands Prix; to bring international credibility, the historic transatlantic link with the Indianapolis 500 was maintained. Although this anomaly continued until 1960, the respective technical regulations continued to move apart. The American teams showed little interest in pitching their highly specialized oval racers against the European opposition and, with one notable exception in May 1952, vice versa.

The manufacturer that emerged as the one to beat immediately after the war was Alfa Romeo, using the 158 (known as the "Alfetta") that had dominated voiturette racing in 1938–39. In short programs in 1946, 1947, and 1948, this car crushed opposition from Delahaye, Gordini, Maserati, and Talbot-Lago with a dream team of drivers that included prewar stars Achille Varzi and Jean-Pierre Wimille. However, Alfa Romeo's financial situation, coupled with the tragic fatalities of both its star drivers, caused it to take a year out in 1949.

When the Alfa Corse team returned in 1950, it faced much more formidable opposition from the new Ferrari enterprise, and this rivalry led to a remarkable surge in the capabilities of the Grand Prix car. The blown Alfa Romeo engine was raced in 1946 with 265bhp, and 5 years later with 425bhp. It powered Giuseppe Farina to the first FIA World Championship, and Juan Manuel Fangio to the second. It would be 26 years before its ultimate output of more than 280bhp/liter was exceeded by a Formula 1 engine (the 1977 Renault V6 turbo).

In October 1951, the FIA announced a new Formula 1 for 1954 for naturally aspirated 2.5-liter engines. Alfa Romeo pulled out immediately. The 158/159 series was clearly at the end of its development potential, and the company balked at producing a replacement chassis and engine for only two seasons. Maserati and Talbot-Lago also decided to withdraw. Mercedes-Benz spiked a 1.5-liter project. BRM and Gordini were underfinanced, and only Ferrari had a viable Formula 1 package for 1952.

GRAND PRIX REGULATIONS

1946–47 *Formule Libre. Fuel: alcohol-based.* **1948–51** *FIA Formula A. Engine piston displacement: 4500cc maximum (naturally aspirated), 1500cc maximum (forced induction). Weight: free. Fuel: free.* **1949** *Reclassified as FIA Formula 1.* **1950** *Race distance: 300km (186 miles) minimum, 3 hours maximum.*

FIA WORLD CHAMPIONSHIP OF DRIVERS

| 1950 | Giuseppe Farina | Alfa Romeo |
| 1951 | Juan Manuel Fangio | Alfa Romeo |

ABOVE: Raymond Sommer contests the opening race of the first postwar season, the Nice Grand Prix in France in April 1946, with an Alfa Romeo 8C-308. Several of these supercharged, 3-liter, straight-eight cars were revived in peacetime and won 16 major Formule Libre races through 1948. Sommer started at the back but had sliced through the 20-car field when a gearbox problem dropped him behind Luigi "Gigi" Villoresi's voiturette Maserati 4CL. However, the 308 won three French events that summer with Jean-Pierre Wimille, and it was the car to beat in the new Argentine Temporada races during the next European winter, with Achille Varzi and South Americans Chico Landi and Oscar Galvez.

OPPOSITE: Louis Rosier's Talbot-Lago T26C has just passed (and partially obscured from view) an irate backmarker on the entry to Tabac corner at Monaco in 1948 as it chases Eugène Chaboud's No. 10 Delahaye 135S. Both manufacturers expected their 4.5-liter, straight-six cars to be competitive in Formula A. However, the pushrod engines ultimately delivered about 240bhp at 5000rpm and could compete only on the basis of superior reliability and fuel consumption. In 1950, the FIA reduced race distances to 300km to assist "atmo" cars, which could run that far without refueling, but by then the blown Alfa Romeos and multicylinder Ferraris were producing over 350bhp. Delahaye withdrew before the new World Championship.

ABOVE: Jean-Pierre Wimille hustles the nimble Gordini 11 through the Station hairpin at Monaco in 1948. Amédée Gordini produced Formula A and B single-seaters in 1947 with works Simca four-cylinder engines, and they were competitive on low-power circuits. Alfa Corse did not enter this race and released Wimille to drive this one to such effect that he led early on. Wimille went to Argentina with Gordini early in 1949 and was killed during practice for a Temporada race in Buenos Aires. Gordini ran Robert Manzon and Maurice Trintignant in 1949–50 before developing his own Simca-branded DOHC engine in 1951. Supercharged for Formula 1 racing, it was unreliable and Simca ended the relationship.

ABOVE: The first Ferrari to participate in a Grand Prix was a 166 Spyder Corsa sports car with its cycle-style mudguards removed. It was owned and driven in the 1948 Monaco Grand Prix by Count Igor Troubetskoy, a French-domiciled Russian aristocrat who, handily for his racing budget, was married to Woolworth heiress Barbara Hutton. Framed here by the railway bridge at the Portier corner, he is about to be lapped by Luigi Villoresi's Maserati. Later he was punted out of the race when being lapped by Louis Chiron's Talbot-Lago on its way to second place. Troubetskoy entered several races with this car, but it was never competitive.

OPPOSITE: Giuseppe Farina grins broadly as he reaches the finish line at Monaco in May 1948, securing an emphatic victory in the inaugural Formula A Grand Prix with his works-supported Maserati 4CL. An evolution of Ernesto Maserati's 1939 voiturette, the lightweight 4CL was equipped with a blown DOHC four-cylinder engine reliably developing 220bhp at 8000rpm. It was already a popular "customer" race car, and 24 were built. Maserati constantly released a range of development engine suspension and braking components to its favored teams. The 4CL could not win when Alfa Corse was about, but this was the model's 23rd victory in significant events since the war.

ABOVE: Nino Farina meets Princess Charlotte of Monaco and her son the year before Rainier ascended the throne of the principality upon the death of his grandfather, Prince Louis. A doctor of engineering, Farina won here in 1948 as a Maserati-supported independent, and also raced during this season for Enzo Ferrari, who had run him in Alfetta voiturettes in 1938–39. Rainier had not yet begun his efforts to establish a status for the Monaco Grand Prix ranking alongside that of the major events in France and Italy. This race was not contested by the works Alfa Romeo team, which hired Farina to lead its World Championship program 2 years later.

ABOVE LEFT: A black weekend for motor racing began when Achille Varzi was killed in his Alfa Romeo 158 in wet practice for the 1948 Grand Prix of Europe, on the wooded Bremgarten circuit near Berne, Switzerland. This is the opening lap of the race. In the foreground are Raymond Mays (B-type ERA), George Abecassis (Alta), and Gianfranco Comotti (Talbot-Lago 150C, bringing up the rear). On the third lap, Christian Kautz, who had raced for both Auto Union and Mercedes-Benz before the war, was mortally injured in an accident involving two other Maseratis driven by his Scuderia Plate teammate, Emanuel de Graffenreid, and another former Silver Arrows driver, Scuderia Milano's Luigi Fagioli.

ABOVE RIGHT: Driving for Eugenio Minetti's Scuderia Ambrosiana, which had a close technical relationship with Maserati, Alberto Ascari (pictured) and "Gigi" Villoresi raced the new 4CLT/48 for the first time against the all-conquering Alfetta on the Bremgarten cobbles in the 1948 Grand Prix of Europe. The 160mph 4CL Tubolare, the first project undertaken by Maserati under its new owner, Adolfo Orsi, was built on an innovative, ladder-frame chassis with tubular cross-bracing. Ascari had won on its debut in the San Remo Grand Prix that June. Its four-cylinder, 16-valve engine was equipped here with two-stage supercharging, and almost 300bhp at 7500rpm. Ascari finished fifth but Villoresi was a fighting third, splitting three Alfettas.

ABOVE: Jean-Pierre Wimille emerged as the fastest postwar Grand Prix driver. The winner of seven international races between 1932 and 1937, all but one with Bugattis, he was signed by Alfa Corse in 1946 at the age of 39. He is pictured winning the 1948 Grand Prix de l'ACF at Reims, his Alfa Romeo 158 equipped for the first time with two-stage supercharging, which boosted its output from 265bhp to 340bhp at 7500rpm, and its top speed to 170mph. Wimille had to make five pit stops in this race, three of them unscheduled to take on water after his radiator had been holed by a flying stone. Team orders saved his day.

OPPOSITE: Jean-Pierre Wimille spent the prime of his life fighting a guerrilla war against the Nazi occupation of France, but survived—unlike his fellow Grand Prix drivers and Resistance heroes, Robert Benoist and William Grover-Williams, who were both shot by the Gestapo. Wimille's Bugatti 59/50B won the first postwar race in Paris in September 1945, and he was an apposite winner of the Coupe de la Résistance in the French capital in 1946, with an Alfa Romeo 8C-308. His nine victories for Alfa Corse included the 1947 Swiss and Belgian Grands Prix, and the 1948 French (pictured) and Italian Grands Prix. He died the following January, a World Champion in all but name.

 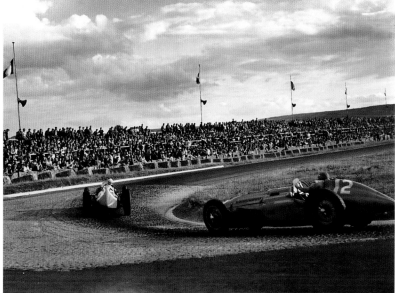

OPPOSITE: The perimeter roadways of the decommissioned former RAF bomber base at Silverstone made an ideal racing circuit, and they were first used for a major event in October 1948. The starting grid for the British Grand Prix was on what is now the short straight between Abbey and Bridge corners. The 25-car field did not include Alfa Corse's cars, and was numerically dominated by British privateer entries such as Sam Gilby's Maserati 6CM, the backmarker in the photograph. Scuderia Ambrosiana's quasi-works Maseratis arrived after qualifying, and Luigi Villoresi and Alberto Ascari had to start from the back. They were 1-2 inside three laps, and stayed there.

ABOVE LEFT: Emanuel de Graffenreid's Maserati 4CLT, starting strongly from the second row of the grid, leads Alberto Ascari's V12 Ferrari 125 and the rest of the 20-car field at Bremgarten in 1949. Graffenreid was swiftly repassed, and the Swiss Grand Prix was contested by Ascari and Nino Farina, until the latter's Maserati lost oil pressure. Luigi Villoresi, his Ferrari fitted here with a long-range fuel tank, took over the lead when Ascari stopped for fuel, but he needed a quick pit stop before the end. Ascari repassed him to lead the Scuderia's 1-2, first time out with two-stage supercharging that lifted power to 305bhp at 7500rpm, and maximum speed above 160mph.

ABOVE RIGHT: Louis Chiron leads "Levegh" (Pierre Bouillon), both in 145mph Talbot-Lagos, on the way to his last major victory, at Reims in 1949. That year's Grand Prix de l'ACF was a sports car event, but this race was also staged as the Grand Prix de France. The Talbot and Darracq brands had been acquired before the war by Italian-born businessman Antonio "Tony" Lago, who had resumed racing with the 1939 MC90 single-seater. The MC90's 4.5-liter straight-six was retained for the new Talbot-Lago T26, which won many minor events. Chiron used superior (9mpg) fuel consumption to race here nonstop, and he defeated faster but thirstier Ferraris and Maseratis.

ABOVE: Alberto Ascari led Giuseppe Farina and Luigi Villoresi in a 1-2-3 for Scuderia Ferrari in the 1949 BRDC International Trophy race at Silverstone. The Ferrari 125 was the first so-named single-seater to be built after Enzo Ferrari had established his own marque in 1946. The car was designed by Gioachino Colombo, the engineer he had hired on Alfa Romeo's behalf in 1937 to produce the voiturette Alfetta, and was powered by a supercharged, 1.5-liter, 60deg V12. Armed with 230bhp at 7000rpm, it debuted in the 1948 Italian Grand Prix in Valentino Park, Turin, and Farina scored Ferrari's first victory 7 weeks later in an Italian Formule Libre race at Garda.

OPPOSITE: The focus of Italian adulation after the 1949 Grand Prix of Europe is Alberto Ascari, the newly famous son of a famous father. His popular flag-to-flag victory with a Ferrari 125 followed successes earlier in the summer at Bremgarten and Silverstone. This was the first international Grand Prix staged since the war on the impressive Autodromo Nazionale at Monza. The venue was extensively refurbished in 1938–39, when the art deco grandstand was built, but fell into a state of disrepair in wartime. Funding was made available to restore it in the summer of 1948, and it reopened with a victory by Jean-Pierre Wimille's Alfa Romeo that October.

ABOVE: The first FIA Formula 1 World Championship gets under way in front of more than 100,000 spectators at Silverstone in 1950. The 360bhp Alfettas are surging ahead of their rivals, and Luigi Fagioli (center) and Juan Manuel Fangio have the edge over Nino Farina. Fangio's car was halted by an oil leak that eventually caused an engine failure, but Alfa Corse secured a 1-2-3, Farina winning from Fagioli and Reg Parnell. The Maseratis of B. Bira, Louis Chiron, and Emanuel de Graffenreid failed to finish, leaving the minor places to reliable atmo Talbot-Lagos driven by Yves Giraud-Cabantous and Louis Rosier—both two laps behind.

OPPOSITE: Nino Farina is flanked by Luigi Fagioli (at right) and Reg Parnell on the first World Championship "podium" after their Alfa Romeos had dominated the Grand Prix of Europe. All three were veterans by today's standards. Farina went on to trigger a multiple crash in the next race at Monaco, but also to win again at Bremgarten and Monza, becoming the inaugural World Champion at the age of 44. He finished with a three-point advantage over Juan Manuel Fangio, who won at Monaco, Spa, and Reims. Fagioli (now age 52) had four second places and was third in the championship. For 39-year-old Parnell, this was a one-off drive.

ABOVE LEFT: An accident at the narrow Tabac corner, caused by seawater breaking over the harbor wall, took out half the field on the opening lap of the 1950 Monaco Grand Prix. Giuseppe Farina spun, and his Alfa Romeo 158 (at left) was struck by Froilán Gonzalez's Maserati 4CLT (center), involving seven other cars. Juan Manuel Fangio, in the lead on his second lap, could not see that the track was blocked as he sped toward the scene, but he noticed that no one in the crowd was looking at him. He slowed his Alfetta and tiptoed through the wreckage. Here Alberto Ascari (at right) is following with the second-place Ferrari 125.

ABOVE RIGHT: No wonder Scuderia Ferrari mechanics winced when they saw burly Jose Froilán Gonzalez bullying their 375. Here he is, straining every muscle of man and beast, securing the Scuderia's maiden Grand Prix victory at Silverstone in 1951. The atmo 375, designed by Aurelio Lampredi to replace the blown 125, was based on a 4.5-liter, 60deg V12, developing 350bhp at 7000rpm. Debuted at Monza late in 1950, it became a contender in 1951 when uprated to 380bhp at 7500rpm. Alberto Ascari was stopped by a gearbox failure in this race but generously declined the team's offer to bring in Gonzalez so that he could take over the leading car.

OPPOSITE: A 26-car grid stands ready for the 1951 Grand Prix of Europe at Reims. At the front are the Alfa Romeos of Juan Manuel Fangio and Nino Farina and Alberto Ascari's Ferrari, with Gigi Villoresi's Ferrari and Consalvo Sanesi's Alfa behind. The last cars built to the 1948–51 formula were extremely potent. Alfa Romeo's blown straight-eight now reached 9300rpm and produced 425bhp. The tanks of the latest 159 evolution held 300 liters of fuel 98% composed of methanol, consumed voraciously at 1.6mpg. The Ferrari's atmo V12 had less power but allowed it to race lighter (carrying 195 liters) with fewer fuel stops. Fangio took over Luigi Fagioli's 159 to win this race.

OPPOSITE: BRM designer Peter Berthon steps forward as Reg Parnell makes a pitstop en route to fifth place in the 1951 British Grand Prix at Silverstone. The all-British BRM project suffered through the involvement of no fewer than 160 component suppliers and was race-ready far too late. The concept was overly complex, including an oleo-pneumatic suspension system and a supercharged, 1.5-liter V16, designed to develop 400bhp at over 10,000rpm. The BRM P15, capable of 180mph, was also the first Grand Prix car to be fitted with disc brakes. The sister P15 of Peter Walker finished seventh here, but, when BRM took three V16s to Monza, none survived qualifying due to mechanical frailty.

ABOVE: Juan Manuel Fangio clinches his first World Championship by winning the Spanish Grand Prix that closed the 1951 season. This former tractor mechanic burst onto the European racing scene in 1948, age 37, with his own Scuderia Argentina Maseratis. He was signed by Alfa Corse for 1950 and won six races, including three championship rounds. He led throughout the 1951 FIA series after winning at Bremgarten, but Alberto Ascari's Nürburgring and Monza victories brought the Ferrari driver into the frame. Fangio went to Barcelona leading Ascari 27-25. They qualified first and second, Ascari on the pole. The Ferrari led at first but was hampered by tire degradation, finishing fourth.

CHAPTER 6
HIATUS
1952–1953

Going into 1952, the Formula 1 World Championship race promoters were faced with a Ferrari walkover. Some nonchampionship grids had been bolstered with cars complying with Formula 2, which was booming. It was suggested that, pending implementation of the new 2.5-liter formula in 1954, the FIA should adopt the "junior" 2-liter category for its World Championship. Ferrari had no objection, having an extremely competitive Formula 2 car and correctly anticipating that the outcome would be the same.

The two seasons of the Formula 2 World Championship were very strong in terms of variety, involving 15 different constructors. AFM, Alta, Aston, Cisitalia, Connaught, Cooper, ERA, Ferrari, Frazer-Nash, Gordini, HWM, Maserati, and Osca contested Grands Prix in 1952, as well as Veritas and other BMW special builders from East Germany. All but four of these continued in 1953.

These seasons were not strong, on the other hand, in terms of competition. All but one of the World Championship races fell to the classy Ferrari 500. This exceptional Formula 2 car won a grand total of 38 events during 1952 and 1953.

Juan Manuel Fangio warmed up for 1952 by winning six of seven Formule Libre races in the South American Temporada with Ferrari, before presenting himself at Modena to lead Maserati's European program. But the works team did not contest the first Formula 2 Grand Prix at Bremgarten, which was won by Piero Taruffi for Ferrari. That day, Alberto Ascari was otherwise occupied—qualifying for the Indianapolis 500.

OPPOSITE: Alberto Ascari turns his Ferrari 500 through the La Source hairpin at Spa, heading for victory in the 1952 Belgian Grand Prix in a 1-2 with Nino Farina. Aurelio Lampredi's four-cylinder DOHC Formula 2 engine developed 170bhp at 7500rpm, and its 150-liter fuel tank could take the 500 nonstop through the contemporary race distances of about 300 miles. The car also had excellent weight distribution, achieved by locating the four-speed gearbox under the driver. During the Formula 2 World Championships, the 500 was uprated to 200bhp at 7500rpm. It won every race it contested except two nonchampionship events and the final Grand Prix of the 2-liter formula.

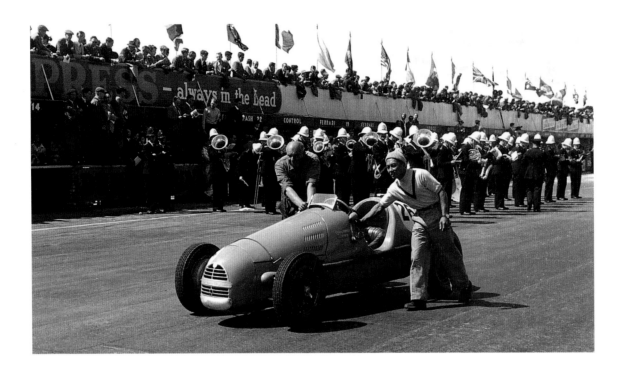

A few events were still being run for Formula 1 cars, and Ferrari was participating with its 375 model. The Scuderia used this 4.5-liter V12 car to make the only serious attempt by a Grand Prix team to score World Championship points at Indy. Ascari failed to finish at the Brickyard and went to the next round at Spa without a point against his name. He won the Belgian Grand Prix—and the remaining five races.

Maserati's 1952 challenge was blunted when Fangio broke his neck in a crash during a nonchampionship race at Monza in June. Ferrari's strongest opposition actually came from the newly developed, straight-six Gordini. Maserati upped its game in 1953, substantially improving its six-cylinder A6GCM and signing alongside Fangio his Argentine compatriots, Froilán Gonzalez and Onofre Marimon. To little avail. Ascari again won all Ferrari's victories except when Mike Hawthorn prevailed in his famous, wheel-to-wheel duel with Fangio at Reims, and Nino Farina defeated Fangio again on the Nürburgring. Fangio was not to be denied: it was his Maserati that finally broke Ferrari's monopoly of Grand Prix victories in the last World Championship Formula 2 race at Monza.

Behind the scenes during these two seasons, a number of serious new 2.5-liter projects were under development. It was time for the new Formula 1.

GRAND PRIX REGULATIONS

1952–53 *FIA Formula 2. Engine piston displacement: 2000cc maximum (naturally aspirated), 500cc (forced induction). Weight: free. Fuel: free.*

FIA WORLD CHAMPIONSHIP OF DRIVERS

1952	*Alberto Ascari*	*Ferrari*
1953	*Alberto Ascari*	*Ferrari*

OPPOSITE: Accomplished privateer driver B. Bira helps to push his six-cylinder, 170bhp Gordini 16 onto the grid before the 1952 British Grand Prix at Silverstone. Amédée Gordini had lost his works engine deal with Simca at the end of the previous season, but, even so, this car was an occasional thorn in the sides of Ferrari and Maserati. A week before this race, Jean Behra's Gordini 16 had inflicted a rare defeat on the Ferraris in the nonchampionship Grand Prix de la Marne at Reims, but this French challenge to the dominant Italian constructors faded in 1953.

ABOVE: Mike Hawthorn (foreground) and Juan Manuel Fangio are engaged in the most famous duel of the two Formula 2 World Championship seasons, neck-and-neck in the lead of the 1953 Grand Prix de l'ACF. Hawthorn had earned his Ferrari contract in 1952 with fourth place in the rain at Spa with a Cooper-Bristol, and third at Silverstone. He and Fangio ran much of the fast Reims road course like this, young Hawthorn in awe of the former World Champion—until he saw him glancing across with a broad grin on his face. In the last corner, Hawthorn's Ferrari pulled ahead of the Maserati and held on to win by a second.

OPPOSITE: Juan Manuel Fangio's Maserati A6GCM has made the best start in the 1953 German Grand Prix on the Nürburgring, chased by the Ferrari 500s of pole position winner Alberto Ascari and Mike Hawthorn. Ascari was soon past Fangio and was leading comfortably on the fifth lap when his Ferrari abruptly parted company with its right front wheel. His teammate, Nino Farina, came through to win from Fangio and Hawthorn. Ascari ruined his brake drum driving back to the pits and took over Luigi Villoresi's car, but he could finish no higher than eighth. This race was contested by 34 Formula 2 cars, 10 of them from communist East Germany.

ABOVE LEFT: Alberto Ascari has changed and packed up his gear as quickly as possible after his disappointing run in the 1953 German Grand Prix, and he is making for the Nürburgring car park. Enzo Ferrari had recruited Ascari from Maserati in 1949, and he had won Formula 1 races with the 125 and the 375, with which he had finished second in the 1951 World Championship, before his extraordinary run of success in the two Formula 2 Grand Prix seasons. Ascari achieved a total of 17 victories with the Ferrari 500 in 1952–53, including 11 in championship events. Both his titles were won by comfortable margins.

ABOVE RIGHT: The last Formula 2 Grand Prix in 1953 produced a classic Monza slipstreaming battle between the Italian-driven Ferraris of Nino Farina and Alberto Ascari, and the Argentine-driven Maseratis of Juan Manuel Fangio (leading) and Onofre Marimon, who was a lap down. This struggle went to the Parabolica on the last lap. Ascari, then leading the group, spun in avoiding the lapped Connaught of Jack Fairman. Farina braked hard to miss his team leader and was hit by Marimon, and Fangio emerged onto the finish straight as a wide-eyed winner. Farina and Ascari got going again and made it to the line still ahead of their teammates, Gigi Villoresi and Mike Hawthorn.

CHAPTER 7
LAST OF THE DINOSAURS: 1954–1960

N one of the constructors that were attracted by the new Formula 1, which included Lancia and Mercedes-Benz, were tempted by the supercharged 750cc alternative to the atmo 4500cc solution (although BRM looked at it closely). The 2-liter Formula 2 engines were capable of almost 100bhp/liter at the end of 1953, so the new formula promised 250 to 300bhp.

Ferrari based the four-cylinder 625 on its super-successful 500 Formula 2 car, while Maserati retained its straight-six for its otherwise new 250F. Ferrari introduced its purpose-designed but ill-handling 553 *Squalo* (Italian for "shark") at Spa, and Mercedes-Benz made a winning comeback in the third Grand Prix, at Reims. Connaught—one of the first small British "special-builders"—arrived with its own chassis powered by a proprietary Lea-Francis straight-four engine at Silverstone 2 weeks later. Vanwall came with another four-cylinder car at Monza in September, and Lancia with its potent V8 D50 in the final round in Spain in October. Clearly, this was the start of a successful formula. It would ultimately be extended through 1960.

Mercedes-Benz dominated in 1954–55, powering Juan Manuel Fangio to the championship in both years. It then withdrew as a consequence of an appalling accident at Le Mans, where one of its sports-racing cars, driven by "Levegh," flew into the crowd and killed more than 80 spectators. This incident caused the cancellation of the 1955 Grands Prix in France, Germany, and Switzerland—and, indeed, a ban on motor racing in Switzerland that remains in place today.

Lancia also withdrew at the end of the 1955 season, for cost reasons. Its hardware was taken over and further developed by Scuderia Ferrari. The so-called Lancia-Ferrari held the upper hand in 1956, when Fangio won his fourth title, and it was raced for three seasons. It was replaced in 1958 by the

OPPOSITE: Before Mercedes-Benz was ready, Juan Manuel Fangio began 1954 with Officine Maserati. He won in Buenos Aires and again here at Spa after a 5-month gap (during which Ferrari and Maserati traded nonchampionship victories). Fangio has just passed Mike Hawthorn's Ferrari 625. The multitubular chassis of the new 250F, created by Gioachino Colombo and developed by Giulio Alfieri, was fitted at first with a 240bhp evolution of the A6GCM/53 engine. This DOHC straight-six was steadily uprated to 270bhp at 8000rpm in 1957, when Alfieri also introduced a V12, developing 320bhp at 9500rpm. The 250F was the most popular customer Formula 1 car of the period, and more than 30 were built.

V6-powered 246 Dino, which took Mike Hawthorn to the championship and saw out the formula. Maserati sold its 250F to several independent entrants and also operated a works team that won the title with Fangio in 1957. The following season, Maserati left its reputation in the hands of privateers for the duration of the formula. Vanwall became a force in 1957, when it scored its maiden win at Aintree, and in 1958 it won the inaugural International Cup for Constructors. BRM returned with a more effective program in 1956 and won its first race 3 years later.

Connaught, which produced the first car to achieve a Formula 1 victory using disc brakes (with Tony Brooks in a nonchampionship race at Syracuse in 1955), raced with Lea-Francis and Alta engines until financial difficulties intervened in 1959. HWM competed occasionally in 1954–55, Aston Martin in 1959, American constructor Scarab in 1960. But the outstanding new constructors of this era were Cooper and Lotus, the British special-builders that both operated works teams and sold many customer cars.

Cooper, which had built effective front-engined Formula 2 cars, entered its first five Grands Prix in 1957 with a four-cylinder Coventry-Climax engine mounted behind the driver of its T43 chassis. This small, light car, developed from Cooper's 500cc Formula 3 concept and the first Grand Prix design with this layout since the Auto Union of 1939, unexpectedly won the first two races of 1958. That year, while granting a request from the fuel suppliers for the mandatory use of commercially available gasoline (for promotional reasons), the FIA reduced race distances. Big fuel tanks were no longer required, and the rules favored small cars. Cooper carried off both championships in 1959 and 1960 with Jack Brabham.

Team Lotus entered Formula 1 in 1958 with a front-engined car, but, as the decade closed, it emerged as a new force due to the innovative mid-engine chassis ideas of its founder, Colin Chapman. Apart from a hollow victory for Ferrari at Monza, all the races in the final season of the 2.5-liter formula were won by either Cooper or Lotus. The FIA's announcement of a 1.5-liter Formula 1 for 1961 clearly called for small, precise racing cars. Chapman saw a glittering future. He was right.

GRAND PRIX REGULATIONS

1954–60 *FIA Formula 1. Engine piston displacement: 2000cc minimum, 2500cc maximum (naturally aspirated), 500cc minimum, 750cc maximum (forced induction). Weight: free. Fuel: free.* **1958** *Fuel: 100–130 octane AvGas petroleum. Race distance: 300km (186 miles) or 2 hours minimum, 500km (310 miles) maximum.*

FIA WORLD CHAMPIONSHIP OF DRIVERS

1954	*Juan Manuel Fangio*	*Maserati & Mercedes-Benz*
1955	*Juan Manuel Fangio*	*Mercedes-Benz*
1956	*Juan Manuel Fangio*	*Ferrari*
1957	*Juan Manuel Fangio*	*Maserati*
1958	*Mike Hawthorn*	*Ferrari*
1959	*Jack Brabham*	*Cooper-Climax*
1960	*Jack Brabham*	*Cooper-Climax*

FIA INTERNATIONAL CUP FOR CONSTRUCTORS

1958	*Vanwall*
1959	*Cooper*
1960	*Cooper*

LEFT: Alberto Ascari put his Lancia D50 on the pole on its debut in the final 1954 race in Barcelona, but both he and Luigi Villoresi were out inside 10 laps. The spaceframe D50, designed by Vittorio Jano (now 62 years old), was powered by a load-bearing V8, putting 260bhp at 8200rpm through a five-speed transmission. The car's outstanding features were its pannier fuel tanks located between the front and rear wheels on both sides. During races, these eliminated the detrimental effects of weight loss on front-rear balance and also had aerodynamic benefits. Ascari won two nonchampionship races in 1955 before pitching his D50 into the sea at Monaco. He swam to safety but was killed 2 weeks later testing a Ferrari sports car at Monza.

ABOVE: Stirling Moss (No. 12) and Juan Manuel Fangio reach the finish line at Aintree in the 1955 British Grand Prix, heading Karl Kling and Piero Taruffi in a crushing 1-2-3-4 by the open-wheel version of the Mercedes-Benz W196. Moss led the last 65 laps with Fangio in his mirrors. Fifteen W196 chassis were built as an engineering team, under Rudolf Uhlenhaut and Hans Scherenberg, experimented constantly with the wheelbase dimension and many other developments. The W196 won 9 of 12 races entered; it failed to win in the other 3 due to unsuitable "streamliner" bodywork and tire deterioration at Silverstone in 1954, and rare mechanical failures at Pedralbes in 1954 and in Monaco in 1955.

OPPOSITE: Mike Hawthorn, signed to lead the revived BRM team in 1956, catches the attention of the Silverstone crowd by taking the lead from the Lancia-Ferraris of Juan Manuel Fangio (No. 1) and Peter Collins (No. 2) at the start of the British Grand Prix. Hawthorn staved them off for 15 laps but was then stopped by a transmission oil leak. Tony Brooks (No. 24) had a lucky escape when the throttle on the other BRM P25 jammed and it somersaulted and caught fire. Stirling Moss's Maserati (No. 7) broke its rear axle, and Fangio came through to win from Collins, who finished the race in Alfonso de Portago's car after his own lost oil pressure.

OPPOSITE: Juan Manuel Fangio and Beba, the vivacious love of his life, emerge happily into the rain from the 1956 British Grand Prix prize-giving party. Fangio, burned by a fuel leak at Reims a fortnight before, raced at Silverstone against doctor's orders, but his victory brought him into contention in his title defense after wins at Spa and Reims by teammate Peter Collins. Fangio took over the series lead by winning on the Nürburgring. When Fangio's steering broke in the final round at Monza, Collins generously sacrificed his own title aspirations by handing his third-place car to Fangio at his tire stop.

ABOVE: Stirling Moss secures Vanwall's maiden World Championship victory at Aintree in 1957. Moss was leading from pole position when his engine began to misfire, and the team called in an unwell Tony Brooks from sixth place so they could swap cars. Moss's brilliant driving brought him 3 seconds closer to the leaders on every lap, and he came through to win after the clutch exploded on Jean Behra's Maserati, and Mike Hawthorn's Ferrari punctured a tire on the debris. At right, Roy Salvadori prepares to push his works Cooper T43, its gearbox broken, across the finish line to claim fifth place.

ABOVE LEFT: Tony Vandervell holds aloft the Grand Prix of Europe trophy, celebrating his team's victory at Aintree in 1957 with Tony Brooks (left) and Stirling Moss. The London-based bearings manufacturer was a director of Norton, and he entered Formula 1 in 1954 with a straight-four based on its single-cylinder motorcycle engine design. After contesting six Grands Prix in 1954–55, he commissioned Colin Chapman to design a new car for a full 1956 program, during which Harry Schell scored points with fourth place at Spa. Now all the effort was bearing fruit: Vanwall scored two more wins in 1957, and six more in 1958 landed the inaugural International Cup for Constructors.

ABOVE RIGHT: Juan Manuel Fangio completes the astonishing drive that clinched his 1957 title with his 24th and final victory, in the German Grand Prix. The 14.2-mile Nürburgring had been resurfaced and Fangio's pole position was 26 seconds under his own lap record—but qualifying established that his rear tires would not go the race distance. Maserati team manager Nello Ugolini secretly started him on a half-full fuel tank and planned a pit stop. Fangio built up a lead of 28 seconds, but after the stop rejoined almost 50 seconds behind the Ferraris of Mike Hawthorn and Peter Collins. Fangio threw caution to the winds, attacking curves in a higher gear than he had used all weekend, driving one lap in 8 seconds under his pole time. He almost put both the Ferraris off the track in repassing them and won by 3.6 seconds. Later, 46-year-old Fangio remarked that he had taken so many risks that he couldn't sleep for 2 days. He retired after contesting the first two races of 1958.

OPPOSITE: The Vanwall team qualified its cars 1-2-3 for the 1957 Italian Grand Prix at Monza. Stuart Lewis-Evans (No. 20) is on the pole, flanked by the sister cars of Stirling Moss and Tony Brooks, and Juan Manuel Fangio's works Maserati 250F in the fourth position at lower right. The Ferraris were outpaced in this race and could not reach a thrilling, place-swapping battle between these four cars and the new V12 Maserati of Jean Behra (No. 6). The cars of Brooks, Lewis-Evans, and Behra eventually wilted under the pressure. Moss, who had defeated Fangio the previous month in the only World Championship race staged at Pescara, held on to deny him again.

OPPOSITE: Graham Hill's dwarfed Lotus 12 harries privateer "Chico" Godia's Maserati 250F out of the Eau Rouge corner as they dice in the midfield during the 1958 Grand Prix of Europe. Team Lotus had entered Formula 1 with this little car a month earlier at Monaco, where Cliff Allison had exploited its precise handling to finish sixth. He had repeated that result at Zandvoort, and the devastatingly simple Lotus continued to rock the establishment, even on the much faster circuit here at Spa. Allison scored the first World Championship points for Colin Chapman's team by finishing fourth, but Hill lost his 2.2-liter, four-cylinder Coventry-Climax engine at half-distance.

ABOVE: Tony Brooks's Vanwall pit board shows him with a 41-second lead over Mike Hawthorn's Ferrari, and his previous lap time was 4 minutes, 2.6 seconds. This 130mph victory at Spa in 1958 set a new record for a European road race. It was one of six wins that brought Vanwall the inaugural Constructors championship but not the Drivers title: Brooks and Stirling Moss each had three victories with the team, but Moss lost out by a single point despite winning the finale in Casablanca. Stuart Lewis-Evans died after crashing Vanwall's third car in Morocco, and Tony Vandervell lost heart for Formula 1. After entering one race in both 1959 and 1960, Vanwall was gone.

ABOVE LEFT: Mike Hawthorn repeatedly broke the lap record as he reduced Tony Brooks's lead at Spa in 1958, but his Ferrari was still more than 20 seconds behind at the end. The winning Vanwall finished the race just as its transmission jammed in third gear, and the Ferrari engine blew after crossing the line. Recalled by Ferrari to replace Juan Manuel Fangio the previous season, Hawthorn was now a force with the disc-braked 246, whose 65deg V6 gave him 270bhp at 8300rpm. He won next time out at Reims and ended the 10-race season in Casablanca with his fifth second place, becoming the first World Champion with only one victory.

ABOVE RIGHT: The 1958 season included the inaugural Portuguese Grand Prix on the 4.6-mile Boavista street circuit on the Oporto seafront, where the mid-engine revolution is pictured in full swing. Tony Brooks is the Vanwall driver under unwelcome pressure from Maurice Trintignant in Rob Walker's privateer Cooper-Climax. Trintignant shone on street circuits and had won at Monaco earlier in the season. This day, he again outran the newer works Coopers of Jack Brabham and Roy Salvadori, and he was past the Vanwall before it spun out of the race. Trintignant drove to sixth place, only to be slowed by a faulty suspension damper.

ABOVE: Peter Collins drains a welcome pint after he and his good friend Mike Hawthorn finished 1-2 for Ferrari in the 1958 British Grand Prix at Silverstone. The 6-foot, 2-inch Hawthorn liked to race with a bow tie, and French fans called him *Papillon* (butterfly). Hawthorn, who had won at Reims a fortnight before, was devastated by Collins's fatal accident on the Nürburgring 2 weeks after this photograph was taken. He reluctantly completed the season and found himself the new World Champion when he finished second in Morocco, whereupon he retired from racing. He was killed in a traffic accident in January 1959.

ABOVE: A young autograph hunter at the top left stalks Jack Brabham at Monaco in 1959. Brabham, a dedicated engineer/driver, left Australia for England in 1955 and was given a chance to race a Formula 2 Cooper in the British Grand Prix while working in the firm's factory near London. He saved enough money to race a Maserati 250F occasionally in 1956, and he was the driver when Cooper made its proper Formula 1 debut at Monaco in 1957, running third and finishing sixth after pushing his sick T43 to the line. Brabham, now armed with the new T51, is preparing to beat Tony Brooks's Ferrari 246 to secure his maiden Grand Prix victory.

OPPOSITE: Jack Brabham hurls his works Cooper T51 at a fast left-hander at Sebring during the inaugural United States Grand Prix that ended the 1959 season. Coventry-Climax now had a full 2.5-liter iteration of its torquey, four-cylinder FPF engine, producing about 240bhp at 6750rpm for the lightweight cars of Cooper and Lotus. Brabham ran out of fuel on the last lap but pushed his car more than 500 yards to the finish line to claim fourth place. Victory was inherited by his teammate, Bruce McLaren (following here), from Maurice Trintignant in Rob Walker's Cooper. Tony Brooks's third place for Ferrari was not enough to deprive Brabham of the first of two back-to-back championships.

ABOVE: Jo Bonnier scores BRM's maiden World Championship victory with a second-generation P25 at Zandvoort in 1959. After the disarray that had characterized its first Grand Prix program, BRM had won with its V16 cars in Formula 1 in 1952–53, and in Formule Libre in 1954. The company was taken over by British industrialist Sir Alfred Owen, who financed Peter Berthon to design a new spaceframe car in 1955, powered by a 280bhp straight-four developed by Tony Rudd. This win came from pole position, but although Bonnier fought off the works Coopers, he inherited it when Stirling Moss's Cooper broke its gearbox.

OPPOSITE: Jack Brabham's race-leading works Cooper-Climax has long gone, but Maurice Trintignant, Stirling Moss, and Bruce McLaren entertain 150,000 spectators, assembled at Aintree for the 1959 British Grand Prix, with a vigorous contest for second place. Later the gearbox of Rob Walker's privately entered Cooper malfunctioned, leaving Trintignant with only two ratios, and he was passed by both his pursuers. In an exciting finish, Moss, hired by the British Racing Partnership team to race its BRM P25 in two midseason events, held off the 22-year-old driver of the other works Cooper T51 to claim the place. Trintignant finished fifth behind Harry Schell's works BRM.

ABOVE LEFT: A week after his company had won its maiden Grand Prix victory—albeit with Stirling Moss at the wheel of Rob Walker's privately entered Lotus 18—Colin Chapman offered 24-year-old Jim Clark a race in a factory car in the 1960 Dutch Grand Prix at Zandvoort. Clark was immediately on the pace, and his debut was memorable for a long duel with Graham Hill's mid-engined BRM P48. The pair are shown here passing the abandoned Cooper of Bruce McLaren on the entry to the big Tarzan hairpin. Their contest ended when the Lotus broke its gearbox. Hill raced on to finish third behind Jack Brabham's Cooper and Innes Ireland's Lotus.

ABOVE RIGHT: Graham Hill consults the list of lap times compiled by his wife, Bette, during practice for the 1960 British Grand Prix at Silverstone. The couple were leading lights in the many social functions held during the Formula 1 seasons in this era. Hill had driven his first 16 Grands Prix with Team Lotus but had now joined Jo Bonnier and Dan Gurney at BRM, which had hastily cannibalized its P25 race cars to join the mid-engine revolution with the P48. In a season that delivered two victories for Lotus, Hill's third place at Zandvoort with the generally unreliable P48 was the only highlight.

OPPOSITE: Phil Hill makes a pit stop at Monza in 1960 with his Ferrari 246, near the end of a season in which Cooper and Lotus had done all the winning. This day, Ferrari's tormentors were absent; incensed by the organizers' decision to use the full Autodromo Internazionale for the Grand Prix of Europe, including its controversial banking, the British teams boycotted the race. In leading Richie Ginther and Willy Mairesse to a 1-2-3 for Ferrari, Hill became the first American to win a Grand Prix since Jimmy Murphy in 1921. This was also the last victory by a front-engined Formula 1 car.

CHAPTER 8
THE GARAGISTES
1961–1965

In the last two seasons of the 6-year, 2.5-liter formula, Cooper had changed the whole Formula 1 picture by winning the championships with small cars bearing off-the-shelf Coventry-Climax engines and Hewland gearboxes behind the drivers. Enzo Ferrari disparagingly referred to the British special-builders as the *garagistes*, but the new 1.5-liter formula not only kept them at front of stage, but swelled their numbers. The formula also established the Grand Prix car as small, nimble, and highly adjustable.

The FIA had again given 2 years' notice of the new rules, which gave Scuderia Ferrari ample time to adjust to the new engine location requirement. Its first mid-engined car, a V6, was testing months in advance of the first Grand Prix at Monaco in May 1961. Stirling Moss brilliantly won that race with a Lotus 18, but the distinctive "sharknose" Ferrari 156 won the other five championship events in the presence of other new cars from BRM, Cooper, and Porsche. Phil Hill became America's first World Champion, but then Ferrari's program was set back for a while by a walkout by its top engineers, led by Carlo Chiti.

In 1962, Coventry-Climax produced a competitive and affordable V8, enabling two more small British constructors, Brabham and Lola, to join the fray. This engine was also used for a development of more significance in the long term: the Lotus 25, which stimulated a new revolution in Grand Prix racing. It made its debut in 1962 at Zandvoort, where its aluminium sheet, monocoque chassis tub attracted immediate attention. Hitherto, all cars had been built up on tubular frames, but this innovation, offering simplicity, strength, and superior torsional rigidity, would be copied by every constructor.

OPPOSITE: Jimmy Clark eyes the apex of the La Source hairpin at Spa during an outstanding drive in the 1962 Belgian Grand Prix, which secured his maiden victory from 12th on the grid. The new Lotus 25, equipped with the latest 195bhp Coventry-Climax V8, was the first car with an aluminium monocoque chassis tub, although it had not yet occurred to its designer, Colin Chapman, to locate the water radiator anywhere other than in the nose. Clark's uncannily precise driving fully exploited the exceptional handling of the 25. He won six races with it that season, including two more World Championship events at Aintree and Watkins Glen.

BRM produced a spaceframe car for 1962 with a fuel-injected V8, with which Graham Hill won the championship in the face of opposition from Lotus and Porsche, and the team remained competitive through 1964–65 with the monocoque P261. But it was Colin Chapman and his go-ahead Team Lotus, enjoying a close relationship with Coventry-Climax, that emerged as the class act in the five seasons of this formula. Leaving Cooper Cars far behind, Chapman's company won 74 of about 180 major races (including nonchampionship events), 17 secured with the Lotus 18, 18 with the 21, 7 with the 24 (which was also powered by a BRM V8), 24 with the 25, and 8 with the 33. Jim Clark won the championship in 1963 and 1965, losing out in an evenly contested 1964 season to John Surtees in the first monocoque Ferrari.

ATS, BRP, De Tomaso, Emeryson, Ferguson (with a four-wheel-drive experiment), Gilby, and other small firms also built cars for the 1.5-liter formula, but the final race, in Mexico, was won by a potentially much more powerful contender. Honda's victory came in its second Formula 1 season and only its third year as an automobile manufacturer.

GRAND PRIX REGULATIONS

1961–65 *FIA Formula 1. Engine piston displacement: 1301cc minimum, 1500cc maximum (naturally aspirated). Dry weight: 450kg (992lb) minimum. Bodywork: open-wheel. Rollover bars compulsory. Fuel: commercially available petroleum. Oil replenishment banned during races.*

FIA WORLD CHAMPIONSHIP OF DRIVERS

1961	Phil Hill	Ferrari
1962	Graham Hill	BRM
1963	Jim Clark	Lotus-Climax
1964	John Surtees	Ferrari
1965	Jim Clark	Lotus-Climax

FIA INTERNATIONAL CUP FOR CONSTRUCTORS

1961	Ferrari
1962	BRM
1963	Lotus
1964	Ferrari
1965	Lotus

ABOVE LEFT: Stirling Moss enters Casino Square in Monaco during the first 1.5-liter Formula 1 race, in which he defeated a squadron of three new V6 Ferraris with Rob Walker's privately entered Lotus 18 Climax. Walker's record with Moss was already exceptional; they had scored the maiden Formula 1 wins for both Cooper (in 1958 in Argentina) and Lotus (in 1960 at Monaco). Walker was courted by Ferrari to run a car for Moss in 1962, but Moss was severely injured at the start of the season. Ricardo Rodriguez and Gary Hocking were killed in Walker's Lotus cars in 1962, but he persevered with Coopers in 1963 and Brabhams in 1964–65.

ABOVE RIGHT: Giancarlo Baghetti can almost taste the champagne as he battles with Porsche 718 drivers Dan Gurney and Jo Bonnier for the lead of the 1961 Grand Prix de l'ACF. Baghetti came to Reims having won minor races in Syracuse and Naples, but this was his first World Championship start. Bonnier—like the other three Ferrari 156 drivers—dropped out of contention, and Baghetti slipstreamed past Gurney on the last lap. He remains the only man ever to win on debut. That October he won another minor race at Vallelunga (in a Porsche). In short seasons with Ferrari, ATS, and BRM cars in 1962, 1963, and 1964, he never looked like winning again.

OPPOSITE: Wolfgang "Taffy" von Trips splashes toward a faultless victory at Aintree in 1961, with teammate Richie Ginther in his wheel tracks. The neat, sharknose Ferrari 156, produced for the new Formula 1 by a team under Carlo Chiti, started out with a 65deg V6 based on the Scuderia's Formula 2 engine. It was now equipped with a 120deg V6, developing more power (190bhp) and designed by Mauro Forghieri to lower the car's center of gravity height. This was the outstanding car of the 1961 season, and its drivers finished 1-2-3 in the British Grand Prix, with Phil Hill having passed Ginther to take second position.

ABOVE: The 1961 German Grand Prix winner, Stirling Moss, cheerfully shares the laurels at the Nürburgring with Wolfgang "Taffy" von Trips. Moss's victory with Rob Walker's Lotus 18/21 was his 16th and last Formula 1 success. His career was closed by a life-threatening accident early in 1962 at Goodwood, in the crushed cockpit of the UDT-Laystall team's Lotus 21 entered by his father, Alfred Moss, and his personal manager, Ken Gregory. Trips had won at Zandvoort and Aintree, and his second place here put him in the lead of the championship, 33-29 over teammate Phil Hill, with Monza and Watkins Glen to come.

ABOVE LEFT: Phil Hill speeds around the banked section of the Monza *autodromo* in the lead of the last Italian Grand Prix for which it was used. Scuderia Ferrari qualified its sharknose cars 1-2-3-4 for this race, points leader Taffy von Trips on the pole ahead of Ricardo Rodriguez, Richie Ginther, and Hill. On the second lap, Trips's 156 collided with Jim Clark's works Lotus 21 on the back straight and, in the ensuing accident, Trips and 14 spectators were killed. Hill drove on to a joyless victory that clinched the 1961 title.

ABOVE RIGHT: Graham Hill celebrates the victory at Zandvoort that began his march to his first World Championship in 1962. Second on the grid for the season-opening Grand Prix of Europe to John Surtees' Bowmaker/Yeoman team Lola, Hill's new BRM P57 was unchallenged after the Lola's suspension broke and transmission problems hampered both Jim Clark's Lotus 25 and Dan Gurney's Porsche 804. The fuel-injected, 190bhp BRM V8 set a new standard, revving to 10,500rpm. That year's Ferrari V6 and air-cooled Porsche flat-eight could go to 10,000rpm, and the Coventry-Climax V8 used by Cooper, Lola, and Lotus to only 9000rpm.

ABOVE: The Monaco Grand Prix is staged on the twisting, undulating streets of Monte Carlo for the 9th time in 1962 as a Formula 1 World Championship event, and for the 20th time since being established in 1929. The race has made Monaco a mecca for beautiful people and, although real wealth has not yet arrived on the Côte d'Azur, there are a couple of serious yachts in the harbor. The founder of this unique race and of the Automobile Club de Monaco, Antony Noghes, was a wealthy cigarette manufacturer who resided in the principality for tax reasons. These days, this is the residence of many Formula 1 drivers.

OPPOSITE: Bruce McLaren's success is filmed by his wife, Pat, as he brings his six-speed, Climax V8-powered Cooper T60 into victory lane after winning the 1962 Monaco Grand Prix. As Lotus ascended during the first half of the decade, John Cooper's technically smart but commercially naive enterprise declined. Jack Brabham left to form his own team, and Cooper lacked the financial resources to match the fierce new development pace set by its rival. This win, secured after Graham Hill's BRM V8 had broken down, was the only one of nine by Cooper this season that counted for the World Championship.

ABOVE: Dunlop executives gather their drivers together for a group photograph before the 1962 German Grand Prix at the Nürburgring. The British company was in its fifth season as a Formula 1 tire supplier, servicing BRM, Cooper, Lotus, and Porsche, and this would be its 38th victory. In the front are (left to right): Jim Clark, car constructor John Cooper, Innes Ireland, Stirling Moss, Graham Hill, Jo Bonnier, Dunlop competitions director Dick Jeffrey, Bruce McLaren, and Dan Gurney. Dunlop had lost its Ferrari contract to Pirelli at the end of the previous season, but again won every Grand Prix in 1962.

OPPOSITE: This might not happen these days: Colin Chapman and his ace Team Lotus driver, Jimmy Clark, undertake a very close inspection together of Lorenzo Bandini's new, uprated Ferrari 156 in the Nürburgring pits in 1962. Ferrari had failed to respond to the arrival of effective new cars from BRM, Lola, Lotus, and Porsche. Fierce internal politics had led to a walkout by many of Ferrari's top engineers, and not even the brilliance of Mauro Forghieri could overcome the weight problems of the 156 when BRM and Lotus came on strong. Ferrari cut short its 1962 program blaming "labor problems in Italy."

ABOVE: John Surtees firmly emphasizes a point to Mauro Forghieri, the 27-year-old technical director of Ferrari, in the Monaco pit lane prior to his first Grand Prix with his new team in 1963. Surtees' stubborn determination to bring focus to the program, and Forghieri's outstanding engineering ability, helped the Scuderia recover from losing many of its engineers before the 1962 championship. Surtees produced a much-needed, morale-boosting win on the Nürburgring 2 months later. Ferrari completed its recovery by landing its second 1.5-liter title the following season, when Surtees became the only man to win World Championships in both 500cc motorcycle racing and Formula 1.

OPPOSITE: The tension shows in Jim Clark's face, as well as disappointment and shock caused by his sudden exit from the 1963 Grand Prix of Europe after 78 laps of the Monaco street circuit. Clark's Lotus 25 started the season opener from pole position and was leading by 16 seconds when its transmission seized. Its rear tires screeching, the car slithered to a smoky halt. Graham Hill's BRM inherited victory, and Clark's bid for the title started badly. Nonetheless, Clark went on to claim 12 victories during the season, including a record 7 in World Championship rounds, 5 of them going away from pole position.

ABOVE: The 1964 Grand Prix de l'ACF was a watershed for the new Brabham team. Formed in 1962, it had won a couple of nonchampionship races in 1963 when Ron Tauranac designed its BT7 around the Coventry-Climax V8. Now Dan Gurney was at hand when Jim Clark's similar engine blew after his Lotus had led 30 laps of the Rouen-les-Essarts road circuit. Gurney delivered Brabham's maiden championship victory, and his ambitious team owner, double World Champion Jack Brabham (pictured), finished third almost on the gearbox of Graham Hill's BRM. Gurney won again in the season finale in Mexico City, and Brabham was on its way.

ABOVE LEFT: John Surtees wins the 1964 German Grand Prix with the Ferrari 158, the Scuderia's first monocoque, powered by a V8 producing 210bhp at 11,000rpm (the design of which was overseen by the legendary Vittorio Jano). Surtees beat Graham Hill to the checkered flag, and the two went on to slug it out for the title all the way to the end of this evenly contested season. Hill was delayed in Mexico City, and Surtees's second place behind Dan Gurney's Brabham clinched it 40-39. Only the best six scores counted, and Hill had to discard two of the points he had scored in his BRM P261.

ABOVE RIGHT: Lorenzo Bandini's second-place Ferrari 1512 is followed through the Station hairpin at Monaco in 1965 by John Surtees's 158, which finished fourth. Ferrari had decided to build two different Formula 1 engines in 1964 but had been unable to introduce Mauro Forghieri's flat-12 (the first fully load-bearing Formula 1 engine) until the penultimate race of that season. With 225bhp at 11,500rpm, the 1512 was ultimately quicker than the 158, but neither could mount a realistic challenge to Jimmy Clark and the Lotus 33. Team Lotus missed this race, running Clark to victory in the clashing Indianapolis 500.

OPPOSITE: The 1965 Belgian Grand Prix at Spa-Francorchamps started in a drizzle, and it was raining hard before the end of the opening lap. From pole position (right), Graham Hill's BRM P261 got down the hill and into the Eau Rouge corner in front of Jim Clark's Lotus 33 and the other BRM of Jackie Stewart, but Clark was the master of the track conditions and was soon in the lead. By the end, only he and Stewart were on the same lap. Hill slipped down the order to finish fifth behind Bruce McLaren's Cooper T77 and Jack Brabham's BT11.

OPPOSITE: The Honda team prepares to send Richie Ginther out of the Zandvoort pit lane in 1965, where he repeated the sixth-place finish he had achieved 5 weeks earlier in securing the company's first World Championship points at Spa. Honda's compact, 60deg V12, first raced on the Nürburgring in August 1964, was built in Japan for a program based in the Netherlands. Transversely mounted in the new RA272 chassis, this was the highest-revving Grand Prix engine yet, delivering more than 220bhp at 12,000rpm. The Formula 1 establishment looked at Honda's record in motorcycle racing and knew that a Japanese victory was not far away.

ABOVE LEFT: Jackie Stewart heads for victory in the Italian Grand Prix, late in his debut Formula 1 season with the 1965 iteration of the P261, BRM's first monocoque. Stewart, fresh from a dominant Formula 3 season with Ken Tyrrell's Coopers, had finished third in only his second Grand Prix, at Monaco, and had followed up with second places behind fellow Scot Jimmy Clark at Spa, Clermont-Ferrand, and Zandvoort. Here at Monza he leads Clark's Lotus 33 and John Surtees's Ferrari 1512 as they turn into the Parabolica. Clark was stopped by a broken fuel pump, Surtees by a clutch failure, and Graham Hill came along to complete a BRM 1-2.

ABOVE RIGHT: Honda closed the 1.5-liter formula with an impressive flag-to-flag victory in Mexico City—the first success for the manufacturer, its tire supplier, and its driver. Richie Ginther's Goodyear-equipped V12 Honda RA272 qualified on the second row but sped past Jim Clark's Lotus 33 and Dan Gurney's Brabham BT11 before the end of the mile-long start/finish straight. Clark's engine blew early on, and Gurney, putting together a late charge, was still almost 3 seconds behind the Honda at the finish. Ginther's teammate, fellow American Ronnie Bucknum, finished fifth behind Mike Spence in the second works Lotus and Jo Siffert in Rob Walker's Brabham-BRM.

CHAPTER 9

RETURN TO POWER
1966–1976

The Formula 1 regulations introduced by the FIA in 1966 were so successful that they endured for 23 seasons. Over the first decade of that period, all the constructors ran 3-liter atmo engines and none even contemplated the 1.5-liter forced-induction alternative. This option was viewed as an inconsequential anomaly in the regulations, in which the FIA saw no need to meddle apart from implementing aerodynamic restrictions, small increases in the minimum weight, and other safety measures.

The FIA had given ample notice of the rule changes in November 1963, but the new formula looked shaky at first. Coventry-Climax, hitherto the accomplished supplier of the British *garagistes*, decided against completing a V16 project, and retreated to its core business—fork-lift trucks. Consequently there were only eight 3-liter engines at the race that opened the 1966 season at Monaco, which was won by a 2-liter BRM V8. But a 3-liter engine did win the 1966 championship: Jack Brabham's Repco V8, based on the versatile Buick/Oldsmobile "stockblock." The reliable Brabham-Repco combination succeeded again in 1967 despite the presence of V12s from Ferrari, Honda, Maserati (with Cooper), and Weslake (with Eagle), and BRM's typically complex H16, which was also supplied to Lotus.

It was the Ford Motor Company that came to the rescue of the independent British constructors that were now desperate for an off-the-shelf engine. Ford's decision to finance the design and development of Cosworth Engineering's purpose-built DFV V8 not only solved the engine supply problems, but also revolutionized chassis design. Team Lotus had an exclusive deal with Ford at first, but yielded to the manufacturer's pressure to release this sensational new engine to McLaren and Tyrrell in 1968,

---

OPPOSITE: Jimmy Clark shows his delight as he embarks on a victory lap at Zandvoort in 1967 after the debut victory of the 185mph Lotus 49 and the Cosworth DFV engine. Clark's teammate, Graham Hill, qualified the sister car on pole position for the Dutch Grand Prix, and led until sidelined by a broken cam-gear on the new V8. It has often been said that Cosworth Engineering's seminal DFV was the best investment Ford ever made in motor racing. It would be used by all the race-winning teams in this preturbo Formula 1 period except BRM, Cooper, Eagle, Ferrari, and Honda.

and Brabham in 1969. When BRM did not take its new V12 to that year's French Grand Prix, the only car not DFV-powered was a solo V12 from Ferrari, which was now maintaining a token presence while concentrating on developing a new flat-12.

With so many cars with identical engines, chassis engineering came to the fore, and especially the new science of aerodynamics. Wings were the subject of unrestricted development until the FIA intervened on safety grounds. For the 1968 Indianapolis 500, Lotus built a four-wheel-drive car powered by a gas-turbine engine, and this project led to short-lived 4WD projects in Formula 1 by Lotus, Matra, and McLaren. Engine specialist Cosworth flirted with becoming a constructor with a 4WD car designed by Robin Herd.

Cosworth then concentrated its resources on making the DFV reliable and saw no need to increase its output substantially until 1971, under new challenges from high-revving 12-cylinder engines built by BRM, Ferrari, and Matra. The Ford-badged engine was uprated in increments from 405bhp to about 465bhp in 1974, and it won all 14 Drivers and Constructors championships that followed its debut season in 1967. An ambitious new flat-12 project by Tecno, an under-resourced Italian Formula 2 constructor, was ineffectual in 1972–73; Matra withdrew at the end of 1972; BRM's challenge faded; and only Ferrari maintained an effective multicylinder program. Ferrari finally defeated the DFV in 1975.

That season was also notable for an event that pushed Bernie Ecclestone, now the owner of the Brabham team, down the road toward taking control of Formula 1. The teams arrived in Barcelona to find the barriers of the Montjuich Park circuit in a dangerously unready state, and a strike was orchestrated by the Grand Prix Drivers Association. The teams, each therefore unable to honor its individual contract with the Spanish promoter, were powerless when their equipment was impounded. The incident confirmed that the Formula One Constructors Association (FOCA), founded back in 1964 by Lotus team manager Andrew Ferguson, was ineffectual. Ecclestone would become FOCA's president in 1978 and would transform it into a powerful political player.

Thanks to the DFV, the 3-liter formula brought a new stability to Formula 1. The engine enabled midfield teams to transform themselves into front-runners, and no fewer than 20 ambitious entrepreneurs and former drivers to become new constructors. These included Tyrrell in 1969, March and Surtees in 1970, Williams in 1972, Ensign and Shadow in 1973, Hesketh, Hill, and Penske in 1974, and Fittipaldi in 1975. It can be argued that the affordability, availability, and reliability of the DFV had the effect of stifling race engine development, but it produced terrific Grand Prix racing.

A French plot was hatched to engineer the DFV's downfall.

GRAND PRIX REGULATIONS

1966–76 *FIA Formula 1. Engine piston displacement: 3000cc maximum (naturally aspirated), 1500cc maximum (forced induction).* **1969** *Weight: 500kg (1102lb) minimum. Wing restrictions.* **1970** *Weight: 530kg (1168lb) minimum. Fuel "bag-tanks" mandatory. Minimum cockpit dimensions. Safety foam in fuel cells.* **1972** *Engine cylinders: 12 maximum. Weight: 550kg (1212lb) minimum.* **1973** *Weight: 575kg (1268lb) minimum. Fuel cell volume: 250-liter maximum. Deformable structure enclosing fuel cell, dry-break fuel-line couplings.* **1974** *Rear wing overhang (behind rear axle centerline): 1000mm maximum.* **1976** *Width: 2150mm maximum. Rear wing overhang: 800mm maximum. Front overhang: 120cm maximum. Tire width restriction. Airbox height and volume restrictions.*

<table>
<tr><td colspan="3">FIA WORLD CHAMPIONSHIP OF DRIVERS</td><td colspan="2">FIA INTERNATIONAL CUP FOR CONSTRUCTORS</td></tr>
<tr><td>1966</td><td>Jack Brabham</td><td>Brabham-Repco</td><td>1966</td><td>Brabham</td></tr>
<tr><td>1967</td><td>Denny Hulme</td><td>Brabham-Repco</td><td>1967</td><td>Brabham</td></tr>
<tr><td>1968</td><td>Graham Hill</td><td>Lotus-Cosworth</td><td>1968</td><td>Lotus</td></tr>
<tr><td>1969</td><td>Jackie Stewart</td><td>Matra-Cosworth</td><td>1969</td><td>Matra</td></tr>
<tr><td>1970</td><td>Jochen Rindt</td><td>Lotus-Cosworth</td><td>1970</td><td>Lotus</td></tr>
<tr><td>1971</td><td>Jackie Stewart</td><td>Tyrrell-Cosworth</td><td>1971</td><td>Tyrrell</td></tr>
<tr><td>1972</td><td>Emerson Fittipaldi</td><td>Lotus-Cosworth</td><td>1972</td><td>Lotus</td></tr>
<tr><td>1973</td><td>Jackie Stewart</td><td>Tyrrell-Cosworth</td><td>1973</td><td>Lotus</td></tr>
<tr><td>1974</td><td>Emerson Fittipaldi</td><td>McLaren-Cosworth</td><td>1974</td><td>McLaren</td></tr>
<tr><td>1975</td><td>Niki Lauda</td><td>Ferrari</td><td>1975</td><td>Ferrari</td></tr>
<tr><td>1976</td><td>James Hunt</td><td>McLaren-Cosworth</td><td>1976</td><td>Ferrari</td></tr>
</table>

LEFT: The first Formula 1 McLaren made its debut at Monaco in 1966, the opening race of the 3-liter formula. After 7 years with Cooper, Bruce McLaren had set up the team at his Can-Am sports-racing car factory. His M2B, equipped with a version of Ford's Indianapolis V8, ran sixth early on but was stopped by an engine failure. McLaren fitted an underpowered Serenissima sports car V8 for the next race and used it to score his team's first championship point at Brands Hatch, but he returned to the deafening American engine to finish fifth at Watkins Glen. Two years later, McLaren was winning races with the Cosworth DFV.

ABOVE: Formula 1 drivers got together to form the Grand Prix Drivers Association in 1961 to represent their collective interests, particularly their contractual and safety concerns, in dealings with the FIA, the team owners, and the race promoters. Here the GPDA is convened at Monaco in 1966 (left to right): John Surtees, Phil Hill, Richie Ginther, Graham Hill, Jackie Stewart, GPDA secretary Peter Garnier, Mike Spence, Jo Bonnier, and Jo Siffert. They are discussing how their views might usefully be expressed in the script of *Grand Prix*, John Frankenheimer's feature film that was made during this season.

ABOVE LEFT: The variety and competitiveness of the 3-liter formula, in only its second season, are evident on the grid for the 1967 Grand Prix de l'ACF, which was held on this single occasion on the Bugatti circuit at Le Mans. Left to right, Graham Hill's Lotus 49 Cosworth V8, Jack Brabham's Brabham BT24 Repco V8, and Dan Gurney's Eagle T1G Weslake V12 are in the front row. Behind them are Jim Clark's Lotus and Bruce McLaren (in a guest drive for Eagle), then Denny Hulme's Brabham, Chris Amon's Ferrari 312 V12, and Jochen Rindt's Cooper T81B Maserati V12. Brabham and Hulme finished 1-2 in this race, and none of the other cars in the photograph finished.

ABOVE RIGHT: Dan Gurney quit Brabham at the end of 1965 to fulfil his ambitions as a constructor, arranging an exclusive deal for a new Weslake V12. Until this engine was ready, the Eagle chassis (pictured on the limit of adhesion during the 1966 Dutch Grand Prix) was fitted with a Climax four-cylinder. The V12 burst onto the scene when Gurney led Richie Ginther to an Eagle 1-2 in the 1967 Race of Champions and, that June, Gurney scored a magnificent victory at Spa. This was the first Grand Prix success by an American car and driver for 45 years, and everyone was thrilled for Gurney – and just as disappointed when Anglo American Racers did not survive beyond 1968.

ABOVE: The variety and competitiveness of the 3-liter formula, in only its second season, are evident on the grid for the 1967 Grand Prix de l'ACF, which was held on this single occasion on the Bugatti circuit at Le Mans. Left to right, Graham Hill's Lotus 49 Cosworth V8, Jack Brabham's Brabham BT24 Repco V8, and Dan Gurney's Eagle T1G Weslake V12 are in the front row. Behind them are Jim Clark's Lotus and Bruce McLaren (in a guest drive for Eagle), then Denny Hulme's Brabham, Chris Amon's Ferrari 312 V12, and Jochen Rindt's Cooper T81B Maserati V12. Brabham and Hulme finished 1-2 in this race, and none of the other cars in the photograph finished.

OPPOSITE: Keith Duckworth (at left) allows a party from BRM to inspect his all-new Cosworth DFV engine and the Lotus 49 in the Zandvoort pits prior to its debut in the 1967 Dutch Grand Prix. Jackie Stewart (holding his helmet), Chris Irwin (here to race a BRM-powered Lotus 25), Mike Spence, and engineer Tony Rudd (wearing an armband, talking with Spence) seem impressed, and so they should be. Installed as a fully stressed, load-bearing chassis member in the purpose-packaged Lotus, the first DFV developed 405bhp at 9000rpm. It won the race with Jimmy Clark, and three more that season including the last two. The DFV went on to fundamentally alter the structure of Formula 1.

OPPOSITE: By 1967, trackside appearances by Enzo Ferrari were becoming rare, but here he is at the Italian Grand Prix with his technical director, Mauro Forghieri. Ferrari was running a solo, 400bhp 312 at Monza for Chris Amon—the best driver never to win a Grand Prix. Both constructor and driver were fourth in the Formula 1 championships in a season scarred by the death of Lorenzo Bandini in a horrific fire at Monaco. These were difficult times for Ferrari, and, as Cosworth developed the DFV, more struggle was to come. Nevertheless, the Scuderia persevered with Forghieri's 12-cylinder rationale throughout the 3-liter formula.

ABOVE: John Surtees had two Hondas to choose from at Monza in 1967 and decided to race the new RA300, which was based on a monocoque commissioned from Lola Cars and powered by a quad-cam V12 producing 405bhp at 11,500rpm. On race day, Surtees beat Jack Brabham in a dash to the finish line, recording Honda's only 3-liter Formula 1 victory. Tragedy befell Honda at Rouen the following year, when it rushed a new, air-cooled V8 car to a premature debut, and Jo Schlesser crashed fatally. Honda pulled out at the end of 1968 and was not engaged in Formula 1 as a chassis/engine constructor for the next 37 years

ABOVE: Exactly emulating Dan Gurney the previous season, Bruce McLaren landed his first victory in a car of his own manufacture in the 1968 Race of Champions here at Brands Hatch, and followed with its first championship victory at Spa. The Cosworth DFV transformed McLaren into a contender with the elegant M7A, and Denny Hulme was persuaded to join his Kiwi compatriot's team. The defending World Champion won at Monza and St. Jovite in September, and, unlike Eagle, this team would go on to great achievements in Grand Prix racing, despite the death of its founder while testing a Can-Am car at Goodwood in 1970.

ABOVE LEFT: The checkered flag is ready for a momentous victory at Rouen in 1968. The Ferrari V12 had won the second race of the 3-liter formula with John Surtees at Spa, and Lodovico Scarfiotti and Mike Parkes had finished 1-2 at Monza, but the latest 312 had been unsuccessful in 1967. A boost to the Scuderia's morale was needed, and it came here from Jacky Ickx. Small, driver-adjustable aerofoils, mounted over the engine bays, had first appeared on the Ferraris at Spa. A month later, Ickx's 312 was thus equipped when it won the Grand Prix de l'ACF. The never-ending quest for aerodynamic downforce was on.

ABOVE RIGHT: Graham Hill and Jackie Stewart went to the 1968 Formula 1 finale in Mexico City with the championship poised 39-36. The "angle of attack" of their high-mounted rear wings was driver-adjustable, and the mechanism on Hill's Lotus 49B relied on rubber straps near the tops of those ridiculous struts. The strap on the left side broke early in the race. However, the other one did a job it had not been designed to do, and Hill won. In any case, Stewart's Tyrrell Matra MS10, which has just lost a brief lead in this shot, was slowed by a faulty fuel pump and eventually finished seventh and out of the points.

ABOVE: Jochen Rindt's Gold Leaf Lotus 49B is pursued by Chris Amon's Ferrari 312 during the 1969 Spanish Grand Prix. The aerofoils fitted by Lotus for the fabulous Montjuich Park road circuit in Barcelona were massive, and the aerodynamic loads caused catastrophic structural failures. Graham Hill was the first to suffer, and, 11 laps later, Rindt was violently pitched off the track at the same spot and into Hill's wrecked sister car. The FIA acted under its safety protocol, under which it needed to give no notice of rule changes. It banned front-mounted high aerofoils and restricted rear wing dimensions—but wings were here to stay.

OPPOSITE: Jochen Rindt converses with Colin Chapman. After Jim Clark's death in a Formula 2 Lotus in 1968, Chapman never had a comparably close relationship with a driver, and he fell out with Rindt over the fragile wings in Barcelona. The career of the Lotus 49 was extended into a fourth season in 1970, alongside the new 72, and Rindt won with both cars. His extraordinary charge with a 49C at Monaco, which pressured Jack Brabham into a mistake on the last corner, was followed by victories with the 72 here at Zandvoort, Clermont, Brands Hatch, and Hockenheim, prior to the tragic accident at Monza that made Rindt the only posthumous World Champion.

OPPOSITE: The 1970 British Grand Prix gets under way at Brands Hatch with Jochen Rindt's Gold Leaf Lotus 72C (right) on the pole, flanked by Jack Brabham's Brabham BT33 and Jacky Ickx's Ferrari 312B. Behind are Jackie Oliver's Yardley BRM P153 and Denny Hulme's McLaren M14D; Clay Regazzoni's Ferrari is nearest the camera. As at Monaco, Brabham had this race in the bag but handed the win to Rindt on the last lap, this time by running out of fuel. The triple World Champion never came close to winning again. Spaceframes were effectively outlawed this season by the FIA's provision for mandatory fuel cells, and monocoques were used by all.

ABOVE: Chris Amon's relentless pursuit of Pedro Rodriguez's BRM P153 at Spa-Francorchamps in 1970 ultimately fell short at the checkered flag by 1 second. March entered Formula 1 this season by using the DFV as the basis of an effective customer race car that was also used by four independent teams. Amon scored points in six 1970 races, and March had high ambitions. However, Jackie Stewart's victory at Jarama earlier in the year with Ken Tyrrell's March 701 (an interim solution while the team completed the first Tyrrell) was the first of only three: Vittorio Brambilla won on the Österreichring in 1975, and Ronnie Peterson at Monza in 1976.

ABOVE: Jackie Stewart's winning Tyrrell 003 lines up at Paul Ricard in 1971 with the latest Ferraris of Clay Regazzoni and Jacky Ickx. Treadless "slick" tires are now being supplied by Goodyear and Firestone. Ferrari had won four of the last five races in 1970 with its new boxer flat-12, and the 312B2, with 470bhp at 12,500rpm, was more than a match for the latest, 440bhp evolution of the DFV. Ickx arrived in France fresh from victory at Zandvoort, but neither Ferrari finished. Apart from a 3-4 on the Nürburgring and a sixth at Watkins Glen, the 312B did not complete another race. Stewart won six times in Tyrrell's first full season.

OPPOSITE: The class of '72 takes the start at Kyalami, with Denny Hulme, at left in the race-winning McLaren M19A, coming up alongside Emerson Fittipaldi's Lotus 72D. Clay Regazzoni has his Ferrari 312B2 between the Tyrrells of defending champion Jackie Stewart and François Cevert. Mike Hailwood's Surtees TS9B, Mario Andretti's Ferrari, Chris Amon's blue Matra MS120C V12, and Ronnie Peterson's March 721 are also in the leading group. The innovative and long-serving Lotus 72 had been introduced in 1970 with an engine airbox and side-mounted radiators allowing the first wedge-shaped nose, and all the other constructors had copied the concept with front-end variations.

OPPOSITE: Jean-Pierre Beltoise secures BRM's 17th and final victory, at Monaco in the very wet 1972 race. BRM persevered with a typically complex, load-bearing H16 until 1969, when it debuted a V12 with 440bhp at 9300rpm and strong top-end performance. Tony Southgate's P153 and P160 designs won in 1970 with Pedro Rodriguez at Spa at 149.9mph, and in 1971 with Jo Siffert on the Österreichring at 131.6mph and Peter Gethin at Monza at 150.8mph— the fastest Formula 1 race ever seen, and the closest finish. But BRM was in a decline that Louis Stanley, acquiring the team from the Owen Organisation in 1975, was unable to reverse.

ABOVE: With five stylish victories for Team Lotus in 1972, Emerson Fittipaldi became the youngest Formula 1 World Champion, at the age of 25, and he held that honor for 33 years. He won the title for a second time in 1974, with three wins for McLaren, but quit this front-running organization at the end of 1975 to race for a new, Brazilian-funded team established by his brother, Wilson. Fittipaldi Automotive's cars were never fully competitive, and this supremely gifted driver spent most of his last five seasons hidden in the midfield. His decision has mystified followers of Formula 1 ever since.

ABOVE LEFT: Having won the inaugural Brazilian Grand Prix for JPS Lotus in 1973, Emerson Fittipaldi opened his scoring for Marlboro Team Texaco in 1974 with a victory from pole position here in his home race at Interlagos, embedding himself forever in the hearts of the fervent São Paulo fans. This was the start of an enduring 23-year relationship between McLaren and Marlboro. The M23, designed in 1973 by a team led by Gordon Coppuck, was the longest-serving McLaren and was raced successfully into a fifth season, winning 20 races including 16 Grands Prix. It took Fittipaldi to the title in 1974 and James Hunt in 1976.

ABOVE RIGHT: Jackie Stewart and François Cevert enjoy the podium ceremonies at Zolder after finishing 1-2 for Elf Team Tyrrell in the 1973 Belgian Grand Prix, outrunning Emerson Fittipaldi's Lotus 72E. Stewart's victory with the Tyrrell 006 equaled Juan Manuel Fangio's career record of 24 in World Championship events, and he went on to make that 27 before the end of this season, from 99 starts. With his second championship clinched and his decision to retire already made, Stewart did not take his 100th start after Cevert, his teammate and natural successor, was killed in a practice accident before the season-closing United States Grand Prix at Watkins Glen.

ABOVE: Hardly a shirt is in sight as Jackie Stewart speeds beneath the packed natural grandstands of the Österreichring on a hot August day in 1973. On this occasion, Stewart's Tyrrell 006 was second behind Ronnie Peterson's JPS Lotus 72E, but this season JYS only twice failed to finish in the points from 14 starts, and he won five times in cruising to his third title. Tyrrell, Lotus, and McLaren won all 15 races in 1973, gaining extra downforce by putting their rear wings on frame extensions aft of the gearbox—a solution eliminated by FIA regulation at the end of the season.

OPPOSITE: Brabham endured four winless seasons until Carlos Reutemann delivered three victories in 1974 (here leading Niki Lauda's Ferrari 312B3 on the Österreichring). The BT44 was an innovative chassis with a rising-rate pullrod suspension system, designed by Gordon Murray for the team's new owner, Bernie Ecclestone. Reutemann and Carlos Pace added a win apiece with the BT44B in 1975, but titles were never in view. Ecclestone sought a partnership with a manufacturer and secured one with Alfa Romeo, which returned to Grand Prix racing in 1976 with a flat-12 for the Brabham BT45. At first this car raced mostly in the midfield, and the Italian engine was unreliable.

ABOVE: Ferrari began a strong resurgence in 1974 and hit the front in 1975, when the latest evolution of its flat-12, producing 500bhp at 12,200rpm, was combined with a transverse gearbox in the compact 312T. Niki Lauda (pictured at Monza), Ferrari's first World Champion since 1964, won 13 Grands Prix over the next three seasons, and Clay Regazzoni and Carlos Reutemann brought the Scuderia's haul to 16. Lauda would likely have had three championships with Ferrari had it not been for a life-threatening accident in the 1976 German Grand Prix, which led to the end of the now impractical Nürburgring Nordschliefe as a Grand Prix venue after 36 seasons.

ABOVE LEFT: Patrick Depailler unnerved the pit lane when he put the unique six-wheel Tyrrell P34 third on the grid on its debut here at Jarama in 1976, outpacing the team's conventional 007. The regulations did not actually say that a car had to have four wheels, and designer Derek Gardner came up with this idea to minimize frontal area and maximize the steering contact patch. It was that rarest thing, a well-kept Formula 1 secret, despite the bespoke Goodyear tires and the involvement of brake system and other suppliers. Jody Scheckter was driving when the P34 scored its only win, in a 1-2 with Depailler at Anderstorp.

ABOVE RIGHT: Niki Lauda abandons his Ferrari 312T2 at Fuji, hoping that James Hunt will finish fourth or lower in the extraordinary race that closed a dramatic 1976 season. Lauda had been so badly injured on the Nürburgring 11 weeks before that he had been given the last rites. Incredibly, he missed only two races. Courageous driving at Monza and Watkins Glen had brought him here still ahead of Hunt, 68-65. Now his courage has given way to a stronger common sense. Lauda was outraged that the Japanese Grand Prix had been started in flooded track conditions that he considered dangerous to the point of lunacy.

OPPOSITE: In the moody presence of the Mount Fuji volcano, James Hunt leads his Marlboro McLaren teammate, Jochen Mass, during the inaugural Japanese Grand Prix in 1976. Soon after the start of the race, twice delayed due to rolling fog and heavy rain, the Fuji International Speedway timing system broke down, eventually causing confusion among most of the teams. Hunt finished the race convinced that he was fourth—but he was third, pipping Niki Lauda to the title by a single point. Mario Andretti's JPS Lotus 77 won by a lap from Patrick Depailler's six-wheel Tyrrell P34. Mass crashed the other M23.

John Player Team Lotus
Valvoline
John Player Team Lotus
Rex Hart
ecial
NGK
John Player Special
Valvoline
NGK
VALVOLINE
John Player Special
John Player Special
OLYMPUS
OLYMPUS
6
Valvoline
Valvoline

CHAPTER 10
THE TURBO ERA
1977–1988

Throughout the 3-liter atmo Formula 1 of 1966–76, it did not occur to the FIA's Commission Sportive Internationale to remove the option for 1.5-liter forced-induction engines. Exploitation of this anomaly certainly occurred to Renault as it developed turbocharging technology in sports car racing. Renault based a 1.5-liter V6 R&D project on its successful Formula 2 engine, and, at Silverstone in July 1977, it made a conspicuously smoky Formula 1 debut. The British independents were highly amused. Not for long....

Turbocharging arrived in Formula 1 at the same time as radial tires and shortly before aerodynamic downforce reached an unprecedented level, following the introduction by Lotus of "ground-effect" aerodynamics. The combination might have produced a generation of cars with mind-boggling performance, but, before the turbos reached their full potential, downforce was restricted by a flat-bottom rule. This was implemented in 1983 by the new Federation Internationale du Sport Automobile (FISA), which replaced the CSI in 1979.

Also in 1979, Renault secured its maiden win, in front of a French crowd at Dijon, and three more victories were added in 1980. Now the other constructors had to scurry to match the Renault's 520bhp output—which meant ditching the 480bhp atmo Cosworth DFV and getting their hands on turbos.

New 1.5-liter engines were introduced by Ferrari and Hart (supplying Toleman) in 1981, by BMW (with Brabham) in 1982, and by Alfa Romeo, Honda, and TAG (a company purpose-formed by McLaren) in 1983. That season, 12 of 15 Grands Prix were won with turbos, and the Cosworth DFV had its 155th and final win—aptly in Detroit, Ford's home town, with Tyrrell.

OPPOSITE: Colin Chapman's press-on engineering team under Peter Wright took the ground-effect concept to another level in 1978 with the shapely JPS Lotus 79. The car's upper-body surfaces were smoothly contoured, and most of its downforce was generated by suction exerted by the airflow through the sidepods and two big venturi. The whole underbody aerodynamic system was sealed by skirts. This car's exceptional cornering performance overcame the 30bhp power deficiency of the latest Cosworth DFV relative to this season's 510bhp Ferrari flat-12. The Lotus 79 was the dominant car, and all the other constructors had no choice but to copy the concept.

The outputs of the turbocharged engines rose steeply as newly available materials resolved daunting heat management problems. For 1984, FISA tried to restrict their performance by implementing a ban on midrace refueling alongside reduced fuel cell capacity, transforming Formula 1 into a "fuel formula." Further reductions in fuel cell volume served only to restrict ongoing power increases. Formula 1 was all-turbo in 1986, when the best engines were capable of over 1300bhp (almost 900bhp/liter) in qualifying specification.

Finally, in 1987, FISA reached agreement with the constructors to control performance and costs, and announced a new formula for 3.5-liter atmo engines for 1989. In the interim, a separate class was introduced for such engines (for which Cosworth returned with its 590bhp, DFV-based DFZ), fuel cell volume was further reduced, and "pop-off" valves were fitted to the turbos. Even under these restrictions, the Honda V6 was raced by Williams in 1987 with 850bhp. In the 23rd and final season of the formula, a new Honda V6 won 15 of 16 races with McLaren.

McLaren took over from Lotus in the engineering vanguard during this period, which produced many important chassis innovations. The teams embarked on increasingly sophisticated aerodynamic programs. Computer-controlled "active" suspension systems, introduced in 1987 (by Lotus and Williams), did not endure because they were only really effective on low-speed circuits, but electronics technology became important with the introduction of data-acquisition and telemetry systems.

The 1981 Concorde Agreement, which resolved a protracted battle between FISA and FOCA over the control of Formula 1, left FISA as the regulatory body and placed the commercial affairs in the hands of the teams' organization, led by Bernie Ecclestone. The financial rewards grew steadily, and the raised stakes produced a new generation of engineers who saw nothing wrong in cheating.

A ride-height regulation was countered by driver-adjustable, hydro-pneumatic suspension systems. The minimum weight rule was countered by the addition of water tanks, ostensibly for the purpose of cooling the brakes, which were emptied as soon as the cars went out on track after being weighed. Strategic pit stops also allowed the cars to race underweight until they were refueled. Fuel volume restrictions were countered by deep-cooling the fuel (and thereby shrinking it) before it was put in the cars. Consequently FISA was compelled to establish an increasingly complex regime of regulations and technical inspection procedures. These stifled innovation and continue to do so.

Many new Grand Prix teams were formed in this period, including ATS and Wolf in 1977, Arrows and Theodore in 1978, Alfa Romeo (returning after a 28-year absence) in 1979, Osella in 1980, Toleman in 1981, FORCE, Minardi, and Zakspeed in 1985, and Larrousse (with Lola chassis) and March (returning as Leyton House) in 1987. The final season of the formula was contested by 18 teams.

GRAND PRIX REGULATIONS

1977–85 *FIA Formula 1. Engine piston displacement: 3000cc maximum (naturally aspirated), 1500cc maximum (forced-induction). Weight: 550kg (1212lb) minimum. Pedal-box protection.* **1979** *Overall length: 5000mm maximum.* **1981** *Weight: 585kg (1289lb) minimum. Ground clearance: 60mm minimum.* **1982** *Cockpit "survival cell" regulations. Weight: 580kg (1278lb) minimum. Road wheels: four maximum.* **1983** *Weight: 540kg (1190lb) minimum. Fuel cell volume: 250 liters maximum. Underbodies: flat-bottoms. Aerodynamic restrictions.* **1984** *Midrace refueling: prohibited. Fuel cell volume: 220 liters maximum.* **1985** *Aerodynamic restrictions. Reinforced footwell, mandatory crash-test.* **1986** *Engine piston displacement: 1500cc maximum (forced induction). Fuel cell volume: 195 liters maximum.* **1987** *Engine piston displacement: 1500cc maximum (forced induction), 3500cc maximum (naturally aspirated, 12 cylinders maximum). Turbocharger inlet manifold pressure: 4.0bar maximum. Weight: 540kg (1190lb) minimum (forced-induction), 500kg (1102lb) minimum (naturally aspirated). Cockpit cell lateral crash-testing.* **1988** *Turbocharger inlet manifold pressure: 2.5bar maximum. Fuel cell volume: 150 liters maximum. Pedals relocated behind front axle line. Static strength tests of survival cell and fuel cell.*

FIA WORLD CHAMPIONSHIP OF DRIVERS

1977	Niki Lauda	Ferrari
1978	Mario Andretti	Lotus-Cosworth
1979	Jody Scheckter	Ferrari
1980	Alan Jones	Williams-Cosworth
1981	Nelson Piquet	Brabham-Cosworth
1982	Keke Rosberg	Williams-Cosworth
1983	Nelson Piquet	Brabham-BMW
1984	Niki Lauda	McLaren-TAG
1985	Alain Prost	McLaren-TAG
1986	Alain Prost	McLaren-TAG
1987	Nelson Piquet	Williams-Honda
1988	Ayrton Senna	McLaren-Honda

FIA INTERNATIONAL CUP FOR CONSTRUCTORS

1977	Ferrari
1978	Lotus
1979	Ferrari
1980	Williams
1981	Williams

FIA WORLD CHAMPIONSHIP OF CONSTRUCTORS

1982	Ferrari
1983	Ferrari
1984	McLaren
1985	McLaren
1986	Williams
1987	Williams
1988	McLaren

ABOVE: Defending champion James Hunt thrusts his McLaren M26 inside Mario Andretti's Lotus 78 in the first corner of the 1977 Dutch Grand Prix at Zandvoort. The Lotus 78 "wing car" used sidepods shaped like inverted wings to create negative lift, with sliding "skirts" to prevent the airflow from leaking out the sides of the car and limiting the aerodynamic effect. Behind are Jacques Laffite in the Matra V12-powered Ligier JS7, Ferrari 312T2 drivers Niki Lauda and Carlos Reutemann, and John Watson in the Alfa Romeo V12-engined Brabham BT45B. The 78 won five Grands Prix, but Lauda won the championship with the more powerful 500bhp Ferrari.

OPPOSITE: Team Lotus boss Colin Chapman has grabbed one of the bottles of champagne and is enthusiastically turning it on his drivers after their 1-2 in the 1978 Belgian Grand Prix at Zolder. This was one of four such results among eight wins by the Lotus 79, from 11 races. Mario Andretti clinched the championship in a restart at Monza after Ronnie Peterson's legs had been broken in a multiple first-lap accident. Peterson's tragic death from unforeseen complications brought poignant memories of 1961, when America's only previous World Champion, Phil Hill, clinched the title after his teammate had been killed, also at Monza.

OPPOSITE: The Brabham BT46B "fan-car," designer Gordon Murray's outrageous answer to the ground-effect Lotus 78 and 79, stands ready for Niki Lauda in the Anderstorp paddock for the Swedish Grand Prix in 1978. The big fan was driven off the flat-12 Alfa Romeo engine, which was too wide for conventional underbody venturi. The fan extracted air from beneath the car to create a partial vacuum, sealed by sliding skirts. This gave the BT46B prodigious downforce but—despite Murray's tongue-in-cheek insistence that the fan's "primary function" was to cool the engine—the fan produced a hail of protests and was judged to be a movable aerodynamic device. The car was banned after winning this race.

ABOVE LEFT: Jacques Laffite (left) has his Ligier JS11 on the pole for the 1979 season-opening race in Buenos Aires, with teammate Patrick Depailler alongside. Guy Ligier entered Formula 1 in 1976 by acquiring the equipment of the defunct Matra Sport operation, including its V12 engines. When he switched his team to the Cosworth DFV, its cars abruptly became competitive and Laffite won here and at Interlagos. Ligier was a front-runner through 1981 and went on proudly to carry the blue of France in Formula 1 with works Matra engines and then Renault, Megatron, Judd, Lamborghini, and Mugen-Honda. After nine wins from 326 races, it was sold to Alain Prost in 1997.

ABOVE RIGHT: Alfa Romeo returned to Formula 1 as Brabham's engine supplier in 1976 and expanded its program, which was led by former Ferrari engineer Carlo Chiti, by building its own chassis in 1979. The distinctive car is pictured on debut by Bruno Giacomelli at Zolder before the Belgian Grand Prix. The flat-12 was replaced by a 60deg V12 (to allow space for ground-effect air tunnels) and in 1983 Chiti (at right, in suit) produced a turbocharged V8. All the engines were unreliable. In six full seasons between 1980 and 1985, during which it also supplied Ligier and Osella, Alfa Romeo rarely looked like winning races, and never did so.

ABOVE: Jean-Pierre Jabouille, Renault Sport's stalwart development driver, bore the many tribulations of the turbo V6 project alone until 1979, when the team was expanded to two cars and his efforts were rewarded with Renault's first Grand Prix victory in 73 years. Here Jabouille vaults off pole position at Interlagos to lead the 1980 Brazilian Grand Prix. From the second row, Gilles Villeneuve is inserting his Ferrari 312T5 between the Renault RE20 and Didier Pironi's Ligier JS11/15. Behind Carlos Reutemann's Williams FW07B and Jacques Laffite's Ligier is René Arnoux's Renault, which won this race and the next one at Kyalami. The turbo revolution is now firmly under way.

OPPOSITE: Gilles Villeneuve's carefree bravado endeared him to millions of Formula 1 fans. After crashing his Ferrari 312T4 when a tire blew during the 1979 Dutch Grand Prix at Zandvoort, he drove it back to the pits in this alarming, disintegrating condition—and at speed. Four races earlier, Villeneuve had prevailed in a fantastic, wheel-banging battle with René Arnoux's Renault to finish second at Dijon. Villeneuve and Jody Scheckter each won three races with the 515bhp T4, which was reckoned by Enzo Ferrari to be the ugliest car ever built in Maranello. The more circumspect Scheckter took the title by scoring points in 12 of 15 races.

OPPOSITE: The sliding skirts of Nelson Piquet's Brabham BT49 hug the track surface during the Long Beach Grand Prix in 1980. Piquet qualified on his first pole position in California, and he landed his maiden victory by leading the race from start to finish. Lotus's ground-effect concept was further advanced this season by Brabham and Williams, and the cars now had stupendous and clearly dangerous cornering performance. FISA announced the mandatory removal of the skirts, and FOCA teams saw this as a deliberate attack on the ongoing competitiveness of the Cosworth DFV. They challenged FISA's power—and the governing body responded by challenging theirs.

ABOVE: Brabham owner Bernie Ecclestone (right) and former March team principal Max Mosley were the prime movers in the FISA-FOCA war, which almost dominated the on-track action in 1980–81. At the head of FOCA, which represented the independent teams (but not Alfa Romeo, Ferrari, and Renault), they took on FISA president Jean-Marie Balestre over his attempts first to ban FOCA from entering into contracts with race promoters and then to take over the commercial affairs of Formula 1. A protracted battle for control was ultimately resolved by the first Concorde Agreement in 1981. A decade later Mosley was the president of FISA, and he and Ecclestone were running the whole show.

ABOVE: Gilles Villeneuve heads down the hill from Casino Square during his winning drive in the 1981 Monaco Grand Prix. This first victory by the new, 120deg Ferrari V6 turbo, which developed 560bhp at 11,500rpm, ended the Scuderia's 19-race winless streak and was followed by another win, at Jarama. Villeneuve qualified his 126CK second on the grid here, and he took the lead when the DFV in Alan Jones's Williams FW07C was smitten by a misfire 4 laps from the checkered flag. Ferrari's 126-series cars were good enough to win the Constructors titles in 1982–83, but the Drivers championship was elusive. Nigel Mansell's Lotus 87 is in the background.

OPPOSITE: Alan Jones is chased by Nelson Piquet through the Mirabeau corner at Monaco in 1980. Their season-long duel produced high-quality racing between Patrick Head's Williams FW07 and Gordon Murray's Brabham BT49, the best ground-effect chassis in a season in which all the teams except Alfa Romeo, Ferrari, and Renault were still using the DFV. Jones ultimately overcame Piquet to win the championship for Williams for the first time, in the season that followed the team's maiden race win. Here at Monaco, he was stopped by a broken differential, and Piquet was beaten into third place by Carlos Reutemann's Williams and Jacques Laffite's Ligier JS11/15.

ABOVE: Alain Prost (Renault RE30) leads John Watson (McLaren MP4), René Arnoux (Renault), and Nelson Piquet (Brabham BT49C) in a four-way battle for the lead at Dijon-Prénois in 1981. Prost held on to secure his maiden Formula 1 victory. The RE30 was designed in anticipation of FISA's ban on sliding ground-effect skirts, and it had to be substantially modified when FISA compromised with the FOCA teams by allowing fixed skirts. Prost made it the car to beat in the second half of the season, adding two more wins at Zandvoort and Monza. It was too late to have any impact on the championship, which fell to Piquet.

OPPOSITE: Nigel Mansell prepares for a practice run at Silverstone in 1981 with a Lotus 87, as a Lotus 88 sits empty in the foreground. The 88 was devised to circumvent a new rule stipulating a 60mm ground clearance for fixed skirts. The rule was unenforceable because compliance could only be checked when the cars were stationary. The other teams, following the lead of Brabham's Gordon Murray, devised hydro-pneumatic suspension systems allowing the drivers to lower the bodywork when they were out on the track. Peter Wright's solution at Lotus was to build the 88 with two chassis, one with softer suspension, allowing airflow pressure to do the same job. It was controversially banned.

OPPOSITE: Gilles Villeneuve's emotions are clear as he shares the podium with Didier Pironi at Imola in 1982. The San Marino Grand Prix was boycotted by most of the FOCA teams after FISA banned the use of their spurious water tanks, ostensibly for cooling the brakes but actually for bringing the DFV cars up to the minimum weight when the empty tanks had been replenished in *parc fermé*. Pironi won the race by blatantly double-crossing his Ferrari teammate. Villeneuve's anger may have been a factor in the dreadful accident that killed this spectacular and charismatic driver in qualifying for the next race at Zolder.

ABOVE: Gordon Murray (at left, back to camera) supervises the first strategic pit stop of the era, servicing Riccardo Patrese's race-leading Brabham in the 1982 Austrian Grand Prix. Brabham had begun its program with BMW 12 races earlier at Kyalami. Such was the consumption of the early engines that, to get through to the finish without refueling, the BT50 had to start with 40 liters more onboard than the team's DFV-powered BT49D. Murray's response was to start the BT50s with half-full fuel cells, bringing them in for fuel and tires at midrace. This was the first time either had gone that far—and Patrese's engine blew soon after he rejoined.

ABOVE LEFT: Nelson Piquet, Brabham, and BMW came to Long Beach in 1983, surprised by the ease with which they had won the opening race in Brazil. The BT52 had been designed hastily after confirmation of the flat-bottom regulation in November 1982. As the season continued, this combination became the one to beat, with Gordon Murray's much-revised B-version of the chassis and a strengthened Weismann transmission. Although rivals were now also using the tactic of midrace pit stops, the BT52B prevailed. In a close finish with Renault's Alain Prost, Piquet became the first man to win the title with a turbocharged engine.

ABOVE RIGHT: Ayrton Senna hunts down Keke Rosberg's Williams FW09 (background), Manfred Winkelhock's ATS D7, and Jacques Laffite's Williams during the 1984 Monaco Grand Prix in a terrific drive that marked him as an exceptional talent. In atrocious conditions, Senna took the unlikely, four-cylinder Hart turbo-powered Toleman TG184 from 13th on the grid to challenge Alain Prost's McLaren-TAG for the lead. Senna was actually in front when the race was red-flagged at the start/finish line and thought he had won, but the result was declared at the end of the previous lap. Crucially for the eventual outcome of the championship, half-points were awarded after the shortened race.

OPPOSITE: Niki Lauda sits in his McLaren MP4/2 in the Interlagos pit lane before its debut race in 1984. The first advanced composite chassis monocoques were built by McLaren and Lotus in 1981, and this era of Formula 1 produced many advances in structural safety; as a result the FIA was able to introduce a range of mandatory crash-testing procedures. For the MP4/2, McLaren designer John Barnard commissioned Porsche to build a turbo V6 to his exact specifications, pioneering total integration of the chassis and powertrain, which subsequently became a fundamental design precept of all racing cars. Lauda led the Brazilian Grand Prix until halted by an electrical failure.

OPPOSITE: Alain Prost corners his McLaren-TAG turbo on his way to winning the 1985 San Marino Grand Prix—only to be disqualified when his MP4/2B was found to be underweight in postrace inspection, handing the win to Elio de Angelis's Lotus-Renault. The new B-version of the McLaren MP4/2 was a refinement of John Barnard's all-conquering 1984 car, equipped with pushrod suspension and other revisions, but the TAG V6 was no longer dominant. This was a highly competitive season in which McLaren had six wins, Ferrari, Lotus, and Williams three apiece, and Brabham one. Prost's first title compensated him for the disappointment of 1984.

ABOVE: Alain Prost tries to make the best of the situation on the Estoril podium after losing the 1984 World Championship by half a point to his McLaren teammate, Niki Lauda. Prost won the season-closing Portuguese Grand Prix, but Lauda's distant second place was just enough. Ayrton Senna was a fine third in this race for Toleman. Also present is FISA president Jean-Marie Balestre, who moved to restrict performance in 1984 by prohibiting midrace refueling and reducing fuel cell capacity. McLaren's TAG V6 engine set new standards in power and fuel management under this fuel formula, and the MP4/2 won 12 of 16 Grands Prix.

ABOVE LEFT: Oblivious to the miserable weather, the JPS Lotus team welcomes Ayrton Senna after he led from flag to flag at Estoril, securing his first Formula 1 victory from his first pole position. This win in the 1985 Portuguese Grand Prix was also the team's first in its new partnership with Renault that equipped the Lotus 97T with works-built turbo engines, ahead of Renault's withdrawal as a constructor at the end of the season. Peter Warr, who ran the team after Colin Chapman's fatal heart attack in 1982, succeeded in snatching Senna from Toleman, and he raced for Lotus for three seasons, winning six races before moving on to greater things at McLaren.

ABOVE RIGHT: Gerhard Berger celebrates victory in the 1986 Mexican Grand Prix, the first for him and the Benetton team. Having bought and rebranded Toleman, Benetton sourced BMW engines prepared by Heini Mader. The focus of BMW's program was Brabham's troublesome "laydown" version of the four-cylinder engine, but the upright engine gave the Benetton B186 winning potential. The car exceeded 217mph at Monza, where the engine delivered as much as 1400bhp for qualifying. Not all this eye-watering grunt could be used on race days, but Berger's drive in Mexico left the dominant drivers of the season, Alain Prost, Ayrton Senna, Nelson Piquet, and Nigel Mansell, far behind.

OPPOSITE: Formula 1 went behind the Iron Curtain 3 years before it was dismantled when the 1986 Hungarian Grand Prix became the first Formula 1 race promoted by a national government. Run on a purpose-built, state-funded road circuit near Budapest, it was watched by 200,000 people. The winner, Nelson Piquet, tried a new differential setup on his Honda turbo-powered Williams FW11 in practice, and he allowed teammate Nigel Mansell to understand that it didn't work; then he raced with it. Behind, the red FORCE team cars of Patrick Tambay and Alan Jones are being lapped by Mansell and Keke Rosberg's McLaren.

OPPOSITE: Ayrton Senna races the Gérard Ducarouge–designed Lotus 99T Honda on the downtown streets of Detroit in 1987. This event produced a second victory for the computer-controlled Lotus Active suspension system. Sensors monitored the car's reactions to the track surface and Senna's every compensation, and a computer under his seat gave instant instructions to an engine-driven hydraulic pump controlling suspension actuators on each corner of the car. The self-leveling and self-damping system was effective on slower circuits, such as Monaco and Detroit. Team Lotus took justifiable pride in these wins, but, in reality, it was in a slow decline that could not be reversed.

ABOVE: Ayrton Senna heads for victory in Montreal in 1988 and his first World Championship. His McLaren MP4/4 was the most effective of all the turbos, superbly packaged by a team under Steve Nichols. The turbo era ended with five seasons, each dominated by a single team: McLaren with TAG in 1984–85, Williams with Honda in 1986–87, and McLaren with Honda in 1988. FISA drastically reduced fuel cell volume and turbocharger inlet manifold pressure in 1988, but Honda responded by producing a new 13,200rpm V6 for one season only, and McLaren broke all the records in winning 15 of 16 races. The lapped car is Piercarlo Ghinzani's Zakspeed.

CHAPTER 11
HIGH ASPIRATIONS
1989–1994

British race engine specialists Cosworth and Judd each produced an off-the-shelf V8 for the new atmo 3.5-liter Formula 1, enabling a raft of new constructors to sign up between 1987 and 1989. The entry reached an unprecedented 20 teams and as many as 39 cars, which had to be culled to 26 (the maximum then allowed to start) by means of a prequalifying procedure. Several very small teams soon fell by the wayside. Ferrari built a new V12 and so did Chrysler-financed Lamborghini, whose project was led by former longtime Ferrari engineer Mauro Forghieri. Lamborghini did not see out the formula, unlike Yamaha, which produced a V8. However, the outstanding new engines were V10s from Honda and Renault.

Honda began the new formula as it had ended the turbo era, and McLaren retained its status as the top team. The 600bhp Ferrari V12 fortuitously won the first race of the new formula, but McLaren and the 685bhp Honda V10 dominated the first two championships. Honda switched to a V12 in 1991 and won another title before Renault's development pace delivered two championships for Williams.

Electronics technology played a major part in this period of Formula 1 with the controversial introduction of "driver aids"—launch control, traction control, automatic gearshifting, power brakes with anti-lock—which rendered long-established driving skills almost obsolete. The FIA attempted to ban them in 1994.

Ford stayed with the V8 concept when it commissioned Cosworth to build a new works engine in 1989, but the engine made little impact until 1993, when it progressed to 720bhp. McLaren used it after the withdrawal of Honda, and Benetton reached a new level of competitiveness. In the final year of the

---

OPPOSITE: Alain Prost takes the lead for Williams at the first corner of the 1993 Brazilian Grand Prix, as his nemesis, Ayrton Senna, places his McLaren MP4/8 in front of Damon Hill in the other FW15C, and Gerhard Berger in his Ferrari F93A. Prost had quit McLaren to get away from Senna, but the two fought all season for the championship. Senna won this battle, but Prost's seven victories ultimately won him the war, and he retired at the end of the season as a four-time World Champion. The black car is J. J. Lehto's Ilmor V10-powered Sauber C12, which had qualified seventh for the new team's second race.

3.5-liter formula, McLaren turned its back on a deal with Lamborghini (which withdrew as a consequence) and turned to Peugeot for works V10 engines, with disastrous results. The Williams-Renault partnership was set back by Ayrton Senna's fatal accident at Imola, and Benetton, Ford's works team, secured its first championship. It was 10 years since the title had been won with any car other than a McLaren or a Williams, or with an engine other than a Honda, Renault, or TAG.

Senna's death came the day after Formula 1 rookie Roland Ratzenberger had been killed—the first driver fatalities during a Grand Prix meeting since 1983. That dreadful weekend in Italy brought an immediate response from the FIA. A package of new safety measures was introduced at minimal notice and the regulatory body decided on a reduction in engine swept volume for 1995, putting Formula 1 back to 3000cc.

The new teams in this period included Jordan in 1991 and Sauber in 1993, the latter equipped with the new Ilmor V10, funded by Mercedes-Benz. After 37 seasons in Formula 1, Team Lotus raced for the last time in 1994.

GRAND PRIX REGULATIONS

1989–94 *FIA Formula 1. Engine piston displacement: 3500cc maximum (naturally aspirated). Fuel: maximum 102RON octane rating.* **1990** *Detachable steering wheel.* **1991** *Wing and rear overhang restrictions. Dynamic test of survival cell.* **1992** *Safety Car.* **1993** *Fuel: commercial gasoline. Rear tire width: reduced from 18-inch to 15-inch maximum. Aerodynamic restrictions.* **1994** *Midrace refueling: allowed. Underbody: 10mm stepped flat-bottom, ride-height compliance checked by plywood plank. Aerodynamic and engine airbox restrictions. Electronic driver aids: prohibited.*

FIA WORLD CHAMPIONSHIP OF DRIVERS

1989	*Alain Prost*	*McLaren-Honda*
1990	*Ayrton Senna*	*McLaren-Honda*
1991	*Ayrton Senna*	*McLaren-Honda*
1992	*Nigel Mansell*	*Williams-Renault*
1993	*Alain Prost*	*Williams-Renault*
1994	*Michael Schumacher*	*Benetton-Ford*

FIA WORLD CHAMPIONSHIP OF CONSTRUCTORS

1989	*McLaren*
1990	*McLaren*
1991	*McLaren*
1992	*Williams*
1993	*Williams*
1994	*Williams*

ABOVE LEFT: Nigel Mansell moved from Williams to Ferrari in 1989 to race a new V12 car designed by John Barnard, and he won on debut in the Brazilian Grand Prix. Barnard pioneered the semiautomatic gearbox on the Ferrari 640, with an electro-hydraulic shifting mechanism activated by paddles on the back of the steering wheel. Mansell won after Alain Prost was prevented from making his second planned tire stop by an inoperative clutch on his McLaren-Honda. Perhaps the mountains were moved: the skyline beyond the Jacarepagua circuit spookily resembles the supine figure of Enzo Ferrari, who had died the previous August at the age of 90.

ABOVE RIGHT: Nigel Mansell nurses a bleeding hand after winning the 1989 Brazilian Grand Prix, his first race for Ferrari. This was Mansell's 14th career victory, and pained facial expressions on the podium had already become part of his personal mystique. Twice the runner-up in the World Championship, Mansell started this season hopeful of his first title, but the 600bhp Ferrari V12 was not up to the job of beating McLaren's 685bhp Honda V10. Alain Prost won the championship from Ayrton Senna, and the early frailty of the new Ferrari transmission kept Mansell in fourth place behind Williams-Renault driver Riccardo Patrese.

ABOVE: Alain Prost and Ayrton Senna were the teammates with the most publicly acrimonious relationship in the history of Grand Prix racing. With McLaren in 1988–89, they won 25 Grands Prix between them. Their rivalry came to an extraordinary conclusion here at Suzuka. Prost's MP4/5 was leading narrowly with 7 laps to go when Senna gave him a stark choice: cede the chicane, or we collide. Prost was ahead in the World Championship by 16 points, with only this race and the Australian Grand Prix still to count. Prost did the math. They collided. Senna is holding his head in his hands and Prost is pretending to be angry.

OPPOSITE: The first victory by the Renault V10 was secured by Thierry Boutsen with an interim Williams FW12C in the 1989 Canadian Grand Prix here in Montreal. The runaway winner of 18 races in 1986 and 1987 with Honda, Williams had endured a fruitless 1988 season with underpowered Judd V8 engines, but the team's exclusive new deal with Renault put it back in the frame. At the end of the season, Boutsen won again in the rain in Adelaide with the FW13 (purpose-built for the Renault engine), and Williams leapfrogged past Ferrari into second place in the Constructors championship. Both were far behind McLaren and Honda.

ABOVE LEFT: Ayrton Senna used his McLaren MP4/5B (foreground) as a battering ram to take Alain Prost's Ferrari 641 out of the 1990 Japanese Grand Prix, exacting a crude and brutal revenge for the incident with Prost at the same circuit the previous season. This time Senna arrived at Suzuka nine points ahead in the championship with the same two races still to count. Senna started from the pole, but Prost made the better start, unknowingly setting himself up as a juicy target at the first turn. The team that benefited from both the Suzuka incidents was Benetton, which won in 1989 with Sandro Nannini and a year later with Nelson Piquet.

ABOVE RIGHT: Ayrton Senna acknowledges the plaudits of the Arizonan crowd after starting his title defense with an easy victory in the 1991 United States Grand Prix in Phoenix. The McLaren MP4/6 was designed by a team led by Neil Oatley for the new Honda V12, which developed 780bhp at 14,800rpm. Senna started on pole position and led all the way. He followed with three more victories, but then Williams won the next five races with its new FW14. The two teams slugged it out all season, but Senna ultimately won his third title, with Nigel Mansell second (again) and Riccardo Patrese third. McLaren beat Williams to the Constructors title 139-125.

OPPOSITE: Alain Prost follows Ayrton Senna as they trudge away from the scene of their collision at Suzuka on the first lap of the 1990 Japanese Grand Prix. Six weeks before, after years of acrimony, these two had reached a reconciliation of sorts at Monza. The incident left Senna as the new World Champion but sullied his reputation, and many onlookers were aghast that no action was taken against him by the race stewards. The Fiat board of directors actually considered pulling Ferrari out of Formula 1. For a year, Senna insulted the intelligence of everyone who saw this incident by denying that his action had been deliberate.

ABOVE LEFT: Nigel Mansell takes his Williams-Renault through the last turn at Magny-Cours, heading for victory in the 1992 French Grand Prix. This race was red-flagged because of rain when Riccardo Patrese was narrowly leading Mansell. It was made clear to Patrese that he would be blamed if the two FW14B cars collided at any stage after the restart, so he theatrically waved Mansell past. The FW14B benefited from Adrian Newey's aerodynamic expertise and an upgraded Renault V10, producing 760bhp at 14,200rpm. It was the dominant car of the season and finished 1-2 six times. Mansell won the first five Grands Prix, and four more victories finally landed the championship.

ABOVE RIGHT: Behind the safety car that has neutralized the 1994 San Marino Grand Prix after a midfield incident on the start line, Ayrton Senna's Williams is followed by Michael Schumacher's Benetton, Gerhard Berger's Ferrari, and Damon Hill's Williams. Senna was leading soon after the restart when he crashed at 190mph at this spot. The car struck a concrete retaining wall, and he died from massive head injuries. Italian law demands that responsibility is taken for fatal accidents, and Williams engineering directors Patrick Head and Adrian Newey were charged with manslaughter. The case remained active for 11 years before they were finally acquitted in May 2005.

ABOVE LEFT: The huge bank of spectators overlooking the Autodromo Enzo e Dino Ferrari gradually fell silent as everyone at Imola began to realize that Ayrton Senna's accident had had serious consequences. On Friday, Rubens Barrichello had been lucky to escape with his life when his Jordan had crashed violently on a qualifying run. On Saturday, rookie Roland Ratzenberger had been killed in his Simtek—the first Formula 1 fatality for 12 seasons. And now this: Senna was taken to the hospital by helicopter, and his death was confirmed a few hours after Schumacher had won the race and the crowd had dispersed.

ABOVE RIGHT: When Ayrton Senna died at Imola in May 1994, bidding for his fourth World Championship at the age of 34, the government in his native Brazil declared 3 days of national mourning. At least half a million people lined the route of his funeral cortege in his home city, São Paulo. At the time, it seemed that Senna's exceptional career achievements might never be equaled: 65 pole positions from 161 starts, 41 victories among 82 podiums. The loss of this world-famous driver sent shock waves throughout motor racing and prompted the FIA to devise a range of new safety measures, which were implemented without delay.

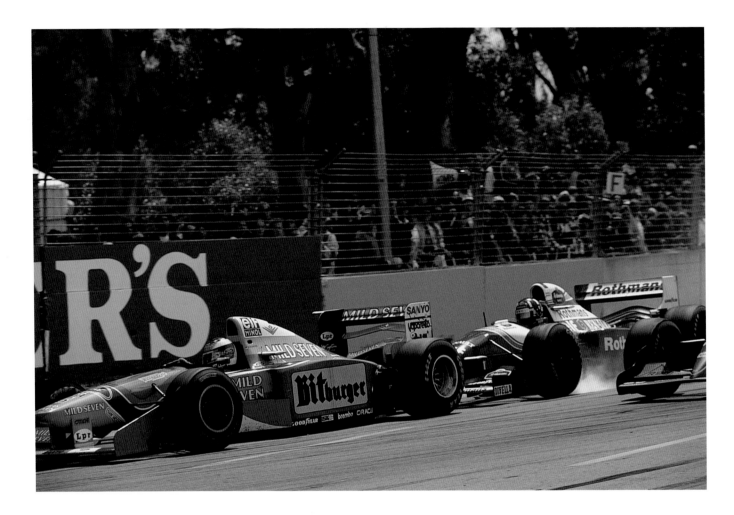

ABOVE: This battle in the 1994 Australian Grand Prix between Michael Schumacher's Benetton B194 and Damon Hill's Williams FW16 was also for the championship. Schumacher had been disqualified after winning at Spa with a car that contravened a ride-height regulation, and he was handed a two-race ban for ignoring a black flag at Silverstone, but the two went to Adelaide with their point scores at 92-91. Schumacher, leading, was out of Hill's view when he ran wide and broke his suspension against a wall. As Hill came alongside, Schumacher turned into him. It was the third time in six seasons that a World Champion was crowned by taking off his only challenger.

OPPOSITE: This spectacular flash fire in the Hockenheim pits during the 1994 German Grand Prix was caused by a partial blockage in Benetton's FIA-supplied "control" fuel rig. It later emerged that the team had removed a filter in order to increase the flow rate into Jos Verstappen's car. The driver and two mechanics suffered minor burns but were not seriously injured. Midrace refueling, prohibited 10 seasons before on the grounds of safety, had been reintroduced to add a strategic element to Formula 1, thereby enhancing the TV show. There were calls for refueling to be banned again, but it was here to stay.

CHAPTER 12
SEEING RED
1995–2005

In the immediate aftermath of the fatal accidents at Imola in 1994, the FIA resolved to reduce power outputs by about 100bhp, to reduce aerodynamic downforce by as much as 30%, and to increase the capability of the chassis structure to absorb energy in impacts. The FIA had to get the agreement of all the teams to implement so many changes to the technical regulations that effectively they constituted a new formula. Consequently the rules were not finalized until September 1994, leaving only 6 months for an entire grid of new cars to be designed, built, and tested before the 1995 season-opening race in Brazil.

Mercedes-Benz, which had returned to Formula 1 in 1994 by funding the Ilmor V10 used by Sauber, entered into a new relationship with McLaren in 1995. At first, however, Benetton and Williams produced the best packages under the new regulations. Both equipped with Renault's new V10, they won all 17 Grands Prix except 2 that fell to Ferrari's V12, and Benetton won a second title.

Williams and Renault won the next two championships, but Ferrari, undergoing an impressive transformation, was a front-runner again in 1997. Renault's withdrawal at the end of that season left Williams without a competitive engine at the same time as McLaren's new partnership with Mercedes-Benz blossomed. It was McLaren that held Ferrari at bay in 1998 and 1999.

In 2000, the FIA reacted to news of several V12 feasibility projects (including one by Ferrari) by making the V10 engine configuration obligatory, on cost grounds. However, the resurgence of Scuderia Ferrari had already gathered an irresistible momentum. Under the leadership of Jean Todt, the team

---

OPPOSITE: Michael Schumacher and Rubens Barrichello race in formation, far ahead of the rest on the Hungaroring in 2001. Under the pressure of the latest engine programs by BMW, Ford, Honda, and Renault, Ferrari surged ahead in the chase for power, and its 2001 engine, the work of Gilles Simon and Paolo Martinelli, developed about 800bhp at 18,500rpm. This 80deg V10 was perfectly packaged in Rory Byrne's F2001 chassis, and the Scuderia's rivals had no answer. Schumacher's 7th victory (of 9) in Budapest was his 51st, equaling Alain Prost's record, and it clinched the title with four races to run. His final points haul of 123 set a new record for one season.

produced a series of superbly packaged cars and achieved a period of domination unprecedented in the history of Grand Prix racing. Over the next five seasons, Ferrari won 57 of 85 races, and Michael Schumacher became the most successful Grand Prix driver ever by adding five more titles to his two with Benetton.

This glittering success by Ferrari was achieved in the face of growing manufacturer involvement in Formula 1. Between 1995 and 1999, Ferrari was the only constructor that also produced passenger cars. Then DaimlerChrysler reportedly paid US$450 million for a 40% stake in the TAG McLaren Group (including its racing team) in 1999. Having backed the formation of Stewart Grand Prix in 1997, Ford paid $80 million to buy the team 3 years later and branded it for Jaguar. Renault paid $120 million for Benetton's team in 2000 and began racing again under its own name in 2002, when another major manufacturer, Toyota, also entered Formula 1.

One effect of the period of Ferrari domination was the certainty of substantial prestige for the manufacturer that could bring it to an end. Ford lost heart for the fight and pulled out at the end of 2004, selling Jaguar Racing to Red Bull. But Renault and McLaren Mercedes persevered and both overcame Ferrari in 2005, when the championship fell to Renault.

As Grand Prix racing prepared for another formula change in 2006, two more manufacturers became operators of wholly owned teams. Honda purchased BAR, which had been created out of the former Tyrrell team 7 years before. BMW abandoned attempts to buy into Williams and instead acquired Sauber. Of the dwindling independent teams, Jordan was sold to MidlandF1, and Minardi—a stalwart backmarker since its debut in 1985—became a second Red Bull team.

GRAND PRIX REGULATIONS

1995–2005 *FIA Formula 1. Engine piston displacement: 3000cc maximum (naturally aspirated). Weight: 595kg (1312lb) minimum (including driver). Width: 2000mm maximum. Aerodynamic restrictions including 50mm stepped flat-bottom. Chassis extension to 300mm in front of pedals. Frontal and side impact tests.* **1996** *Aerodynamic restrictions.* **1997** *FIA Accident Data Recorder. Rear impact test.* **1998** *Width: 1800mm maximum. Grooved tires. Electronic driver aids: prohibited. Front roll-hoop test.* **1999** *Increased impact tests.* **2000** *Engine configuration: V10, maximum five valves per cylinder. Exotic metals prohibited. Survival cell protection measures.* **2001** *Aerodynamic restrictions.* **2002** *Electronic driver aids: allowed.* **2003** *Two-way telemetry: prohibited.* **2004** *Weight: 600kg (1323lb) including driver. Engine deployment: maximum one per race weekend. Launch control and fully automatic gearshifting: prohibited.* **2005** *Midrace tire changes: prohibited (refueling allowed). Aerodynamic restrictions. Engine deployment: maximum one per two race weekends.*

FIA WORLD CHAMPIONSHIP OF DRIVERS

1995	Michael Schumacher	Benetton-Renault
1996	Damon Hill	Williams-Renault
1997	Jacques Villeneuve	Williams-Renault
1998	Mika Hakkinen	McLaren Mercedes
1999	Mika Hakkinen	McLaren Mercedes
2000	Michael Schumacher	Ferrari
2001	Michael Schumacher	Ferrari
2002	Michael Schumacher	Ferrari
2003	Michael Schumacher	Ferrari
2004	Michael Schumacher	Ferrari
2005	Fernando Alonso	Renault

FIA WORLD CHAMPIONSHIP OF CONSTRUCTORS

1995	Benetton
1996	Williams
1997	Williams
1998	McLaren Mercedes
1999	Ferrari
2000	Ferrari
2001	Ferrari
2002	Ferrari
2003	Ferrari
2004	Ferrari
2005	Renault

LEFT: The multinational Mild Seven Benetton Renault team celebrates in 1995 at Suzuka, where Michael Schumacher's victory has just clinched the team's first Constructors championship. Schumacher had landed his second successive Drivers title by winning the previous race at Aida. In the top row, from left to right, are Renault Sport director Christian Contzen, Benetton Group president Luciano Benetton, Japan Tobacco marketing executive Eiji Ito, Schumacher, and team principal Flavio Briatore. A decade had passed since Benetton, after 3 years as a Formula 1 sponsor, had become a constructor by purchasing the Toleman team. These glory days did not continue: Schumacher was off to Ferrari, and Benetton's key engineers, Ross Brawn (second from right in the bottom row) and Rory Byrne, would soon follow him.

ABOVE: Michael Schumacher, watching the lap times during qualifying for the 1995 German Grand Prix from the cockpit of his Benetton, suddenly has his archrival glaring at him from the TV monitor. Damon Hill beat him to the pole by a tenth of a second. As in 1994, these two were engaged in a bitter battle for the championship over most of the season, until Schumacher's string of three wins in the month of October put him beyond Hill's reach. Schumacher won nine times altogether, and two victories by his overshadowed teammate, Johnny Herbert—both after Schumacher and Hill had collided—took Benetton to its first (and only) Constructors championship.

OPPOSITE: In 1996, Damon Hill became the first son of a World Champion to win the title. After taking over as the Williams team leader on the death of Ayrton Senna, Hill had endured two defeats at the hands of Michael Schumacher and now had to cope with another strong opponent in the form of his new rookie teammate, Jacques Villeneuve. Hill's Williams FW18 Renault won the Australian Grand Prix that began the season in Melbourne (pictured), and the next two in South America. He never looked back, and he took his haul to eight victories by season's end. Villeneuve was second in the championship in his debut season.

OPPOSITE: Michael Schumacher, leading Jacques Villeneuve 78-77 in the 1997 championship with 21 laps to run in the final race of the season, squeezes his rival's Williams FW18 toward the grass verge at Jerez. Villeneuve (nearer camera) did not lift and kept on coming—so Schumacher blatantly tried to knock him off the track. It was the Ferrari 310B that ended up in the gravel trap, and Villeneuve was able to continue, clinching the title with third place. Schumacher's claim that he had done nothing wrong was treated with derision, and later a specially convened FIA tribunal stripped him of all the points he had scored during the season.

ABOVE LEFT: Mika Hakkinen's McLaren MP4/13 forces aside Giancarlo Fisichella's Benetton B198 in the first turn of the 1998 Austrian Grand Prix, leading Michael Schumacher's Ferrari F300, Jean Alesi's Sauber C17, and Rubens Barrichello's Stewart SF2. Hakkinen abruptly emerged this season as a genuine star, and he led David Coulthard to an impressive McLaren Mercedes 1-2 on the Österreichring, with Schumacher third. Equipped with an ex-works Renault V10 prepared by Mecachrome and rebranded for Playlife, a Benetton sponsor, Fisichella had started from the pole here due to inconsistent track conditions in qualifying, with Alesi second. They took each other out of the race, while Barrichello retired with faulty brakes.

ABOVE RIGHT: Jordan Grand Prix had its finest hour in 1998 when Damon Hill won in Belgium in a wildly unexpected 1-2 with Ralf Schumacher. Mostly a midfield team since entering Formula 1 7 years before, Jordan never lost ambition and was now equipped with Mugen-Honda engines. These V10s were very effective on the wet track at Spa, where a first-corner incident involved 13 cars. Pictured ahead of the Ferraris of Michael Schumacher and Eddie Irvine, Hill capitalized after the restart when accidents eliminated both Schumacher and McLaren's Mika Hakkinen, and Hill secured his 22nd and last victory. Jordan went on to win at Magny-Cours and Monza in 1999 with Heinz-Harald Frentzen.

ABOVE: Jacques Villeneuve's BAR 01 leads Pedro Diniz's Sauber C18 during the 1999 Australian Grand Prix in Melbourne. After 28 seasons in Formula 1, Ken Tyrrell sold out in 1998 to British American Tobacco, which relaunched the team as BAR and made its debut in this race using ex-works Renault V10s, now race-prepared by Supertec. Each side of the BAR is liveried differently to carry the colors of two different BAT brands. The hype that trumpeted BAR's arrival in Formula 1 was embarrassingly followed by a maiden season in which it was the only team not to score any points. Nevertheless, BAR secured a works Honda engine deal for 2000.

OPPOSITE: Mika Hakkinen (left) and David Coulthard are happy to face the cameras before the 1998 Japanese Grand Prix, the race closing the season in which McLaren won its first title in 7 years. Walking across in front of them is McLaren team principal Ron Dennis, and at bottom right is Mercedes-Benz Motorsport director Norbert Haug. Installed in the first McLaren designed by Neil Oatley with Adrian Newey, who had been lured the previous season from Williams, the latest iteration of the Ilmor V10 developed 770bhp at 16,000rpm. Hakkinen's victory here was his 8th of 16 starts with the MP4/13 and clinched the championship at Michael Schumacher's expense.

ABOVE LEFT: Michael Schumacher's 38th joyful victory leap was already a familiar sight as he celebrated his narrow victory over McLaren's Mika Hakkinen in the 2000 San Marino Grand Prix. Schumacher had been the favorite to win the 1999 championship, but his right leg had been broken in a crash at Silverstone. He had returned for the last two races to assist teammate Eddie Irvine's ultimately unsuccessful title bid. This victory at Imola was Schumacher's third from the first three races of the new season. Now he is sure that he will be the man when Ferrari has a World Champion for the first time since 1979.

ABOVE RIGHT: Mika Hakkinen (left) and Michael Schumacher entertained Formula 1 fans with many exciting battles on the track during their intense and often emotional rivalry between 1998 and 2001, when the McLaren Mercedes driver quit Grand Prix racing with 20 victories to his name. They are pictured together just after the 2000 Belgian Grand Prix at Spa-Francorchamps. Hakkinen is explaining his anger about an outrageous chop by Schumacher that had put him on the grass verge. Hakkinen had taken the lead with a sensational overtaking maneuver a lap later, trapping the Ferrari on the wrong side of Ricardo Zonta's lapped BAR-Honda, and had held on to secure a memorable triumph.

OPPOSITE: Michael Schumacher did not have it all his own way en route to the first of his five titles with Ferrari in 2000. Mika Hakkinen declined to give up his title without a fight and won four races, although his McLaren MP4/15 Mercedes was often outperformed by Schumacher's Ferrari F1-2000. Such was the case here at Monza, where Schumacher gradually eased ahead of his rival and scored the sixth of his nine wins. The Italian Grand Prix was marred when a fire marshal was mortally injured by flying debris in a multicar accident on the first lap, at a point on the circuit where the cars reached 180mph.

ABOVE: Much of the credit for Ferrari's remarkable resurgence was credited to Jean Todt, here on the Magny-Cours podium with 2002 French Grand Prix winner Michael Schumacher. Recruited from Peugeot in 1993 as Ferrari's sporting director, Todt inherited a team that lacked an effective technical department after years of outsourcing in England. He hired the world's best driver and assembled and directed outstanding engineering personnel, transforming the Fiat-owned team's Gestione Sportiva in Maranello into the envy of all its rivals. During the 2002 season, Schumacher won 11 of 17 races and Ferrari's score in the Constructors championship was more than the rest of the field combined.

OPPOSITE: Ralf Schumacher ends a 54-race losing streak for Williams in the San Marino Grand Prix in 2001. The second season of the team's new technical partnership with BMW produced four victories with Schumacher and Juan Pablo Montoya. BMW Motorsport's 90deg V10 was probably the most powerful engine this season and the next: when its engineers broke through the 19,000rpm barrier with an engine built for Monza in 2002, it delivered 880bhp to the Williams FW24 and Montoya drove the fastest ever lap in Formula 1, at 161.423mph. Poor reliability hampered Williams, and that season it won only once, when Schumacher and Montoya finished 1-2 at Sepang.

ABOVE: Mika Salo heads for seventh place in 2002 at Spa-Francorchamps, where the top-end power of the new Toyota V10 could overcome his car's aerodynamic shortcomings. Toyota Motorsport decided to go all the way when it entered Formula 1, undertaking to build its own chassis and engine in a factory in Germany. At the time, only Ferrari was running an integrated program. Having created the biggest team in Formula 1, Toyota devoted the whole of 2001 to testing and development before making its debut in 2002 in Melbourne, where Salo finished sixth. Salo repeated this result two races later at Interlagos, but these were the team's best of the season.

OPPOSITE: Scuderia Ferrari celebrates yet another World Championship double after the Japanese Grand Prix that closed the 2003 season, which contrasted starkly with its almost total domination in 2002. This time, the titles were hard won. The season produced highly competitive racing as Ferrari won eight events, Williams four, McLaren Mercedes two, and Renault and Jordan (fortuitously) one each. McLaren's new star, Kimi Raikkonen, ran Michael Schumacher close for the Drivers title, losing 93-91 when Rubens Barrichello beat him into second place at Suzuka. In the Constructors championship, Ferrari ultimately prevailed with 158 points over 144 scored by Williams and 142 by McLaren Mercedes.

OPPOSITE: Michael Schumacher wins the 2004 Hungarian Grand Prix, clinching a sixth consecutive Constructors championship for Ferrari, and breaking his own record of 11 wins in a single season. Ferrari shocked the opposition that had come close in 2003 by producing a far superior car for the season that followed, with a new chassis, engine, and seven-speed transmission. The F2004—the 50th Formula 1 Ferrari—again took the team out of reach of its increasingly powerful rivals, winning 15 of 18 Grands Prix. After his success in Budapest, Schumacher only won once more in 2004, but it was enough to clinch a fifth straight Drivers championship.

ABOVE: Team McLaren Mercedes principal Ron Dennis confers with his latest Finnish ace, Kimi Raikkonen. Dennis started out in Formula 1 as Jochen Rindt's mechanic at Cooper and Brabham, before embarking on his own Formula 2 project in 1972. This evolved into Dennis's Project 4, which was merged with McLaren in 1980. Dennis soon took over the entire McLaren operation with TAG company founder Mansour Ojjeh, and its Grand Prix cars have carried the MP4 designation ever since. The culmination of Dennis's many achievements during his 25 years in charge is the breathtaking, 50-acre McLaren Technology Centre, part-owned by DaimlerChrysler, in Woking, England, where he was born and raised.

ABOVE: Kimi Raikkonen locks up his front wheels as he wins the charge for the first corner at Monaco in 2005. Raikkonen started from pole position with the McLaren MP4/20 Mercedes, the last McLaren designed by Adrian Newey and generally the fastest car in the 2005 World Championship, with a new engine producing as much as 950bhp at 19,000rpm. Raikkonen was also one of the fastest drivers, but his season was marred by bad luck. He dominated this race until the finish and it was one of seven victories, but Fernando Alonso matched that total and beat Raikkonen to the championship 133-112.

OPPOSITE: Fernando Alonso became the youngest ever Formula 1 World Champion in 2005, at the age of 24. Alonso finished 16 of the season's unprecedented 19 races in the points, winning seven of them, and failed to finish only twice. He is pictured after his victory at Hockenheim, where Nelson Piquet's Brabham BT49C had won the 1981 German Grand Prix when Alonso was 4 days old. Alonso raced his Renault conservatively in midseason to protect his Drivers championship lead and clinched the title with one race to spare.

Postscript

The centenary of Grand Prix racing finds Formula 1 in a strong position. Five of the teams entered for the 2006 World Championship are wholly owned by automobile manufacturers, and a sixth is part-owned. This number is unprecedented in Formula 1 and in Grand Prix racing since 1914.

Through the second half of 2005, all but Ferrari threatened to establish their own "breakaway" championship in 2008 on the expiry of the present Concorde Agreement, which has been redrafted and renewed every 5 years since 1981. The manufacturers wanted greater influence over the sport's commercial affairs, now controlled by the Formula One group of companies under Bernie Ecclestone.

In one sense, then, Grand Prix racing came full-circle over its first 100 years: its story began in 1906 because the companies that built the cars were able to use their influence to change the way motor racing was run.

Grand Prix racing enters its second century with another new set of regulations. Over the 10 years of the 3-liter formula, the power outputs of the front-running engines were increased incrementally from 650 to almost 1000bhp. Yet again the FIA was concerned about performance and costs. Although hampered by a right of veto granted to the constructors in the Concorde Agreement, the FIA finally convinced them to accept a loss of about 200bhp in a switch to naturally aspirated, 2.4-liter V8s. This formula was implemented for the 2006 season, and immediately the teams began to claw back the lost performance by producing engines that could rev above 20,000rpm.

The obstinate practicality of the governing body versus the fierce ingenuity of the teams: Grand Prix racing was ever thus, and always will be.

OPPOSITE: The Renault R25s of Fernando Alonso (right) and Giancarlo Fisichella sandwich Kimi Raikkonen's McLaren MP4/20 as they lead the pack at the start of the inaugural Turkish Grand Prix in 2005. Raikkonen won with Alonso second, Juan Pablo Montoya third in the other McLaren, and Fisichella fourth. However Alonso's victory in the inaugural Chinese Grand Prix that closed the season secured the 2005 double for Renault, edging out McLaren-Mercedes to clinch its first World Championship title as a constructor. It was the 100th year since Renault had won the world's very first automobile Grand Prix, also on Michelin tires.

Acknowledgments

The unique L.A.T. Photographic archive in Teddington, southwest London, has provided every one of the photographs in this book. I know of no other agency in the world that would have been able to do this. I am indebted to Peter Higham, who lives for the vast L.A.T. archive and possesses an amazing knowledge of what it contains, and particularly to Kathy Ager, our expert picture researcher, who is blessed with a wonderful eye for those truly exceptional images. Both went far beyond the call of duty in their dedication to this book, and in their patience with my indecision when presented with so many fine photographs from which to choose so few. I am grateful also for outstanding work by Emma Champion, who lives up to her name in the L.A.T. darkroom. David Bull has been punctilious in his editing, Rachel Bernstein has skillfully turned my English into American, and Tom Morgan has been responsible for the beautiful design.

I am also obliged to many authors and their publishers.

PAGE 240: Returning to Reims after a day's practice for the 1966 Grand Prix of Europe, a Ferrari mechanic hits traffic on the city outskirts and tries not to burn out the clutch of Lorenzo Bandini's 312. The French road circuit had no permanent facilities so, like other teams, Ferrari prepared its cars in a rented garage a few miles from the pits. Grand Prix racing was, indeed, very different 40 years ago. In the race, Bandini was leading by almost half a minute when his throttle cable broke. He got the car back to the pits after rigging up a repair with a hay bale wire, and continued to finish 11th.

Bibliography

For all who engage in motor racing research in Europe, certain well-established sources are indispensable, including two periodicals and one annual:

Autocar (since 1895)
Haymarket Publishing

Autosport (since 1950)
Haymarket Publishing

Autocourse
Hazleton Publishing & Crash Media Group

The indispensable books are:

Grand Prix Data Book
By David Hayhoe & David Holland – Haynes Publishing, 2006

Grand Prix Who's Who
By Steve Small – Guinness Publishing, 1996

International Motor Racing Guide
By Peter Higham – David Bull Publishing, 2003

Record of Grand Prix & Voiturette Racing
By Paul Sheldon & Duncan Rabagliati – St. Leonards Press

I have raided many other fine books for nuggets of information to use in this story, all of which I can recommend for further reading. They are:

All But My Life
By Stirling Moss with Ken Purdy – William Kimber & Co., 1963

Autocourse History of the Grand Prix Car 1945-65
By Doug Nye – Hazleton Publishing, 1993

Autocourse History of the Grand Prix Car 1966-91
By Doug Nye – Hazleton Publishing, 1992

American Automobile Racing
By Al Bochroch – Penguin Books, 1977

Batsford Guide to Racing Cars
By Denis Jenkinson – B. T. Batsford, 1978

Centenary Encyclopaedia of Automobiles
By Graham Macbeth – Temple Press, 1984

Cooper Cars
By Doug Nye – Osprey, 1983

Encyclopædia of Motor Racing
By Anthony Pritchard & Keith Davey – Robert Hale & Co., 1973

Fangio: Life Behind the Legend
By Gerald Donaldson – Virgin Books, 2003

Fangio: Racing Driver
By Olivier Merlin – B. T. Batsford, 1961

Ferrari F1 1948-1963
Edited by Piero Casucci – Libreria dell'Automobile

Ferrari F1 1964-1976
Edited by Piero Casucci – Libreria dell'Automobile

Ferrari F1 1977-1985
Edited by Piero Casucci – Libreria dell'Automobile

Golden Age of the American Racing Car
By Griffith Borgeson – SAE, 1998

Grand Prix Racing 1906–1914
By TASO Mathieson – Connoisseur Automobile, 1965

History of Motor Racing
By William Boddy – Orbis Publishing, 1977

Lotus: Design Revolution
By Doug Nye – Robert Bentley, 1972

Maserati: A Complete History
By Luigi Orsini & Franco Zagari – Libreria dell'Automobile, 1979

Mercedes-Benz: Quicksilver Century
By Karl Ludvigsen – Transport Bookman Publications, 1995

One Hundred Years of the Motor Car 1886-1986
Edited by Marco Ruiz – Willow Books, 1985

Racing Car Development & Design
By Cecil Clutton, Denis Jenkinson & Cyril Posthumus – B. T. Batsford, 1957

Racing Cars & Record Breakers 1898–1921
By T. T. Nicholson – Blandford Press, 1971

Racing The Silver Arrows
By Chris Nixon – Osprey, 1986

Roaring Twenties
By Cyril Posthumus – Blandford Press, 1980

Such Sweet Thunder
By John Blunsden & David Phipps – Motor Racing Publications, 1971

Vanwall
By Denis Jenkinson & Cyril Posthumus – Patrick Stephens, 1975

I have also spent many happy hours bouncing from place to place on the Internet, where Grand Prix racing is served by many excellent (and also many less reliable) historical Web sites. The excellent ones include:

Autosport.com

DDavid.com

Forix.com

GrandPrix.com

RacingCircuits.net

Silhouet.com (Darren Galpin's Motorsport)

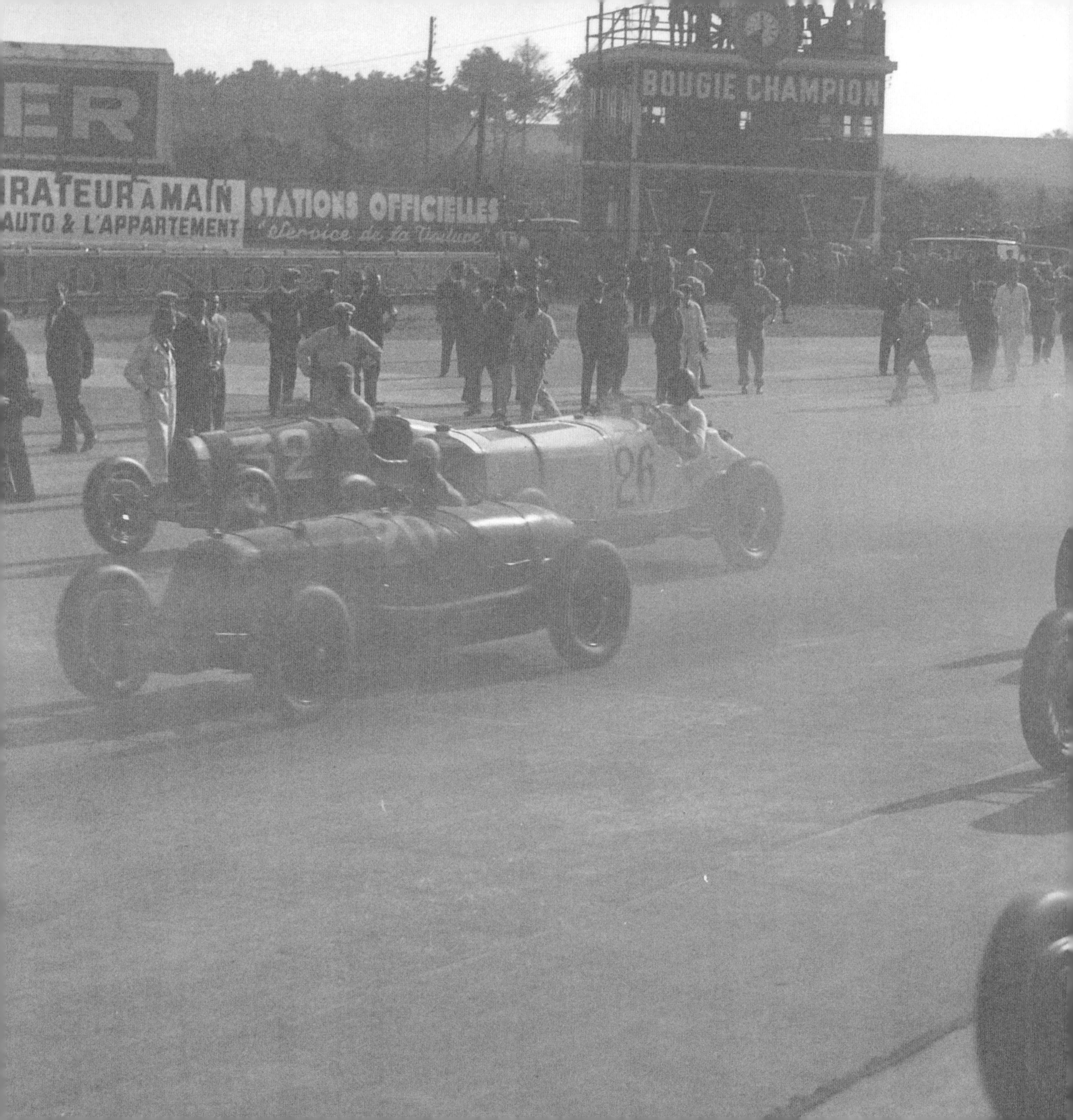
BOUGIE CHAMPION
STATIONS OFFICIELLES
26